FIFTY-FIVE YEARS OF
A FAMILY'S ENTERPRISE

LOVE'S: FIFTY-FIVE YEARS OF A FAMILY'S ENTERPRISE

BY DR. BOB L. BLACKBURN

EDITOR: GINI MOORE CAMPBELL

FIFTY-FIVE YEARS OF A FAMILY'S ENTERPRISE

PREFACE TO THE SECOND EDITION

Five years ago the first edition of this book was released by the Oklahoma Hall of Fame. As the title of book stated, it was the 50th anniversary of Love's Travel Stops and Country Stores, a time to pause, reflect, and describe the DNA of a company that had grown from one little store in Watonga, Oklahoma, to one of the largest travel stop enterprises in the country.

A dominant theme that emerged from that historical odyssey was Tom Love's relentless passion for growth. Every move he made, from finance and organization to personnel and locations, revolved around growth. Tom knew that sustained success depended on finding new opportunities, new directions at every turn that could leverage existing assets and take the company to new plateaus of production and profitability. The minute the Love's team of owners and co-workers were satisfied with their success was the moment the downward spiral might begin.

Instinctively, Tom knew that the glow of the 50th anniversary celebration was the perfect time to shake things up a bit, to set new goals, and push everyone on the team to look for those next plateaus of growth. He had a company culture built on the foundations of teamwork, a deep pool of leaders, and the financial strength to take greater risks and chart new territory in the market place. As you will read in chapter six of this second edition, Tom did not wait long to charge ahead with a bold new plan. Five years later, after staying on pace to double the size of the company by 2020, adding critical pieces to the organization such as Speedco and Trillium, and finding ways to keep the talent pool within the company growing at a remarkable pace, the Oklahoma Hall of Fame and I agreed that the story had to be updated if the lessons learned were to remain guideposts for the future.

Once again, the people at Love's, from top to bottom, took time from their busy schedules to share their memories and archival materials tracing the succeeding five years since the first book was completed. And once again, I was impressed with the individual talent at every level that blends into a company culture of interdependence, trust, and mutual support. I want to thank all of them for providing me with the raw materials that could be formed into a cohesive story of dealing with challenges and seizing opportunities. I also want to thank Shannon Rich and Gini Moore Campbell at the Oklahoma Hall of Fame for including me in this two-part pursuit of Love's history. I promise to use the lessons I have learned to be a better historian, story teller, and public servant.

Most of all, I want to thank the Love family for blazing a path of success built on integrity, teamwork, and faith in the future. The company you have grown helps drive the wheels of the economy and serves the traveling public, but more importantly, your family enterprise creates opportunities for those men and women willing to buy into your vision—your team members scattered from coast to coast. Their success is your success.

Bob L. Blackburn

PREFACE TO THE FIRST EDITION

When Gini Moore Campbell from the Oklahoma Hall of Fame approached me with the prospect of writing a new book in the fall of 2012, I initially said I could not possibly squeeze another project into my schedule. I was as busy as ever at the Oklahoma Historical Society, locked in a multi-year campaign trying to get authorization for a new museum of popular culture, while my weekends and vacation time were already allocated to family, finding and moving to a new old home, and finishing a book manuscript near completion.

Then Gini dangled an enticing lure in front of me. The topic was a history of Love's Travel Stops & Country Stores. As she anticipated, I bit the hook immediately, dismissing all the reasons why I could not take on another project. I wanted to learn more about a company I had watched grow my entire adult life, and I knew the story would be filled with the themes I had been exploring in books and exhibits about the Oklahoma experience.

Despite my interest, I told Gini I needed to make sure I could meet the deadline, which was only one year away. I talked to Jenny Love Meyer, Love's vice president of communications, whom I knew through a museum project that included the story of retail fuel distribution and sales. We talked about the corporate archives, the accessibility to company veterans, and the reasons why she was motivated to help with the research. I not only liked what I heard about resources and coordination, but I also knew I would enjoy working with her.

I talked to the family matriarch, Judy Love. Judy, who is direct and confident, said she would help with the book because it would tell the story of her "Tommy." I would have expected nothing less, plus I knew I would need her energy and sense of urgency if I was to get access to highly motivated business people who had a business to run. Then I talked to Tom Love, the namesake of the company who had been the captain of the ship for the past forty-nine years.

I had met the man behind the smile, but I had never enjoyed the privilege of extended conversations. I immediately liked his candor and congeniality. He listened well and carefully gathered his thoughts before speaking. I explained the research process, which would require a thorough archival expedition to build the bones of the story, followed by a series of interviews starting with him and expanding to others, both inside and outside the company. He said he would open doors and be available.

After we were comfortable with each other, I asked a question that would tip me one way or the other in my decision whether or not to tackle the book. Why would he allocate time and support for a book? He said he did not want a biography of himself. Instead, he wanted a real history of the company, with all of the twists and turns that would not only capture a portrait of how the company had grown, but also generate a better understanding of what had worked well and how those lessons might guide company leadership in the future. He also wanted a history rooted firmly in local, state, and national history. Without the big picture that set the stage for his industry, he said, the lessons learned might capture what happened, but lose the significance of how and why it happened.

Finally, I asked a critical question. I started by stating my belief that the only good history is honest history. If he had made mistakes, if the company had taken the wrong path from time to time, those stories needed to be included alongside the stories of success. Would he object? His response is still crystal clear in my memory. "Bob," he said, "this will be your book. I will share my memories to the best of my abilities and I will point out anything I think is factually wrong, but I will not edit and I will not guide the story." I left Tom's office not only convinced that I should write the book, but that I could not wait to get started.

For the next year, working weekends and vacations, I explored the story of the company. What I found fulfilled all my expectations. Tom was candid and insightful, generous with his time and attention. The only doubt that rose in my mind from our interviews was his consistently positive descriptions of the people he had worked with over the years. Never did he criticize a colleague or a competitor. He might describe a tough decision to replace a person in his organization or trace a hard fought battle with another company, but it was always couched in a positive way that showed a respect for everyone's abilities and motivations. My doubt evaporated as I realized Tom really does see others through a lens of empathy. He likes people.

With a rough timeline from archival records, news clippings, and the interviews with Tom, I added details pulled largely from interviews with current and former employees, people in the industry, and family members, especially Judy, Greg, Frank, and Jenny. Some of the interviews were direct and to the point, such as one session with Tom Edwards, whom Tom Love credits with a large share of the company's success. Others meandered through the maze of memory, such as several insightful sessions with Harold Wells, who started with Love's as a teenager in Watonga and is still part of the company's future.

My interviews with Judy, Greg, Frank, and Jenny added a unique perspective. Each had memories of both the founder and company that started at home, but took shape as they came to understand the industry and the forces that Tom had dealt with since 1964. Especially with the children, their stories started as third-person observers and evolved into first-person narratives of their growing roles in the bigger picture. From my interviews with Judy, I could understand the power of her partnership with Tom and her unwavering confidence that he could climb any mountain.

As I worked through my materials, I added research on the historical forces that posed challenges and created opportunities as the company grew. I explored the world of refineries and the last days of full-service gasoline stations. I tracked the disruption of the the Arab Oil Embargo and federal fuel rationing. I followed the expansion of the interstate highway system and the impact of trucking deregulation. Into the fabric of this narrative story I wove threads of a cyclical economy, changing consumer habits, and the impact of technology. I could see the story unfolding in my mind.

As the work gained momentum, key themes emerged. The first was Tom's belief that growth creates opportunity. From the very beginning, he and Judy shared confidence that they would be successful if they were moving, even if it took them sideways from time to time. For the last fifty years, the story of Love's is the story of steady growth punctuated by a few bursts of explosive growth when exceptional opportunities came within their reach—and even a few times when it was beyond their reach.

Another theme that emerged as I wrote is Tom's ability to share responsibility with others. Like the football player he was in high school and college, he believes in teamwork, and he has always had a knack for finding the right teammates at the right time when the company needed to move in a new direction. It worked with Larry Dillard and Tom Edwards. It worked with his own children, Greg, Frank, and Jenny. In return, Tom earned their loyalty, hard work, and pride in doing a job to the best of their abilities.

As the story unfolded in my mind, I realized that the company had grown in distinct phases as conditions changed and old business models started to lose steam. Each time they reached a pivot point, either from external forces or from internal capabilities, Tom and his leadership team plotted a new course and recharged their efforts to sustain growth. If charted on a graph, the history of Love's would look like a staircase with a series of rounded risers starting straight up, gaining momentum and forward motion with experience, and reaching operational efficiencies on a plateau as competition caught up and conditions changed. I am convinced that another new trajectory is around the corner, as yet undefined, that will add new stories to this narrative history.

This book would have been impossible without the help of others. I want to thank the Oklahoma Hall of Fame, especially president Shannon L. Rich and vice president Gini Moore Campbell, for giving me this opportunity to learn another lesson about Oklahoma history. I want to thank the headquarters staff at Love's, especially Wanda Meador, Michelle Wright, Kathi Stafford, and Mary Lehner, who became my friends as I chased information and scheduled interviews. Most of all, I want to thank the Love family for the trust they showed me as I poked and prodded into the story of their family business. They will remain friends.

Finally, I want to dedicate this book to my wife, Debbie, who sacrificed our family vacations and most weekends over the past year as I pursued my passion to tell another remarkable story.

Bob L. Blackburn, Ph.D.

FIFTY-FIVE YEARS OF
A FAMILY'S ENTERPRISE

A
GOOD
FOUNDATION

1

Tom and Judy Love had a decision to make in the winter of 1963. They were getting by, but barely. He was a former Marine and college dropout grinding through a training program at a full service gasoline station. She was a former secretary, now housewife, with two babies in the home.

Both Tom and Judy knew that a college degree could open doors in the future, but in 1963 with a growing family, the future seemed to be pressing in on them. Tom, a big man with an

In 1963, Tom Love was well prepared for the world of retail gasoline sales thanks to a family legacy of business enterprise. This reproduction of an early gas pump is a symbol of his success.

easy sense of confidence, was anxious to get on with life and knew that Oklahoma's rapidly changing economy offered opportunities to anyone willing to work hard. He wanted a piece of the action.

When Tom Love married Judy McCarthy in 1960, they laid the foundation for a family-owned business and a partnership that would last a lifetime.

The opportunity tempting him to leave the training program was an abandoned service station in Watonga, Oklahoma, that could be leased for little or nothing. Growing up around the world of oil and gas, Tom knew he could buy gasoline in bulk with no money down and nothing due for ten days, enough time to sell the gasoline, pay an employee with the income, and order a second load before the first bill was due. Obviously, someone else had failed to make the service station successful even on those liberal terms, but still it was tempting.

The ability to make such a momentous decision, to pull the trigger when confronted by opportunity, was not easy for anyone, especially a young couple with two babies in a mortgaged home and no money in the bank. While the ultimate decision would be based on Tom's and Judy's confidence in themselves, it also was a reflection of everything in their lives up to that point, especially the imprint of families, mentors, and the state of the general economy. To understand their decision in 1963, as well as the course of their lives after that pivotal year, it is helpful to understand the cultural baggage passed down to them, one generation to the next, and the skill sets they had accumulated on the way to that one moment in history.

While the ultimate decision would be based on Tom's and Judy's confidence in themselves, it also was a reflection of everything in their lives up to that point, especially the imprint of families, mentors, and the state of the general economy.

An aptitude for risk-taking and business investment was a large part of Tom's family legacy. On his mother's side was a grandfather, Thomas E. Vessels, an ambitious farm boy born on the plains of Kansas who went to school through the 5th grade, paid his way through business school in Wichita, Kansas, and moved to Enid, Oklahoma, to make his fortune. Surrounded by rich farmland and booming oil fields, Thomas worked his way up through the ranks to become president of the American National Bank of Enid.

Like many entrepreneurs of his generation, Thomas lost everything in the stock market crash of 1929 and the subsequent Great Depression. He fought back, first as a door-to-door salesman, then as a land man and broker in the oil fields of Texas. Along the way, he accumulated a large personal library and was known among his friends for reciting poetry from memory and singing songs every night for a week without repeating even one. Many of his talents were passed onto his six children, including daughter Margaret, the future mother of Tom Love.

The entrepreneurial roots ran even deeper in the Love side of the family. Most notable was Tom's Chickasaw great-grandfather, Robert Jeremiah Love, the founder of the town of Purcell who seemed to have no fear either when confronted by challenges or tempted by opportunity. That ability was in large part an inherited characteristic wrapped in the dramatic history of the Chickasaw people.

Robert was the grandson of Thomas Love, a Scottish loyalist who fled to the Chickasaw Nation during the American Revolution in 1780 after his father was killed by American patriots in South Carolina. Described by contemporaries as a tall man who spoke

When Robert and Sallie were married, the Chickasaw Nation was still recovering from the devastation of the Civil War in the Indian Territory.

The Chickasaw Nation was a crossroads of commerce after the Civil War. It straddled the wooded east and the prairie west and it was located between settled Texas to the south and Oklahoma Territory to the north after 1889.
Courtesy Chickasaw Archives, Chickasaw Nation.

with a strong brogue, he settled among the large mixed-blood clans of Colberts, Burneys, and Adairs. He married twice, first to Sally Colbert and then to a full blood Chickasaw, Homahota, and between them fathered at least thirteen children.

Out of the first marriage came Benjamin Love, born about 1795, who would use his mixed-blood position between two worlds to earn a reputation as a merchant, farmer, and "the most talented man in the Chickasaw Nation," according to one contemporary source. He married a daughter from the Burney clan and joined

a group of Chickasaw leaders who traveled west to select land for their new home in the Indian Territory. After the removal, he and his extended family settled near the mouth of the Washita River where it flowed into the Red. Benjamin's granddaughter, Sallie Gaines Criner, would be born during the Civil War in 1862.

From loyalist Thomas Love's second marriage came another son, William Love, who moved west to the new Chickasaw Nation in 1844, seven years after the authorized removal. Like his half-brother, William was a gifted diplomat, merchant, and farmer who owned numerous African-American slaves. In 1852 William had a son and named him Robert Jeremiah Love. Robert became an orphan at the age of fourteen and hired out to a rancher herding horses for eight dollars a month. In 1877, after building his personal assets to two cow

When Tom Love's Chickasaw ancestors moved west to the Indian Territory, they found a land where mobility, self reliance, and the willingness to take a risk gave them opportunities to invest in cattle and farming operations.

Non-Indian settlers flooded into the Indian Territory in the 1880s and 1890s as tribal sovereignty suffered a gradual erosion and the American frontier drew to a close. That transition also created opportunities for enterprising Chickasaws.

Purcell was a primary port of embarkation for '89ers who intended to run for land in the Unassigned Lands. These early-day travelers on the interstate highways of that era found services provided by the Love family.

ponies and thirty-two head of cattle, he married fifteen-year-old Sallie Gaines Criner. In a confusing line of Chickasaw genealogy, Robert and his new wife were second half-cousins.

When Robert and Sallie were married, the Chickasaw Nation was still recovering from the devastation of the Civil War in the Indian Territory. Calculated on a per capita basis, the people of the Five Civilized Tribes suffered more loss of life and destruction of property than the people of Virginia from 1861 to 1865. Robert, like his parents and grandparents, coped with the challenges and took advantage of opportunities. Entitled to use as much tribal land as he needed, he built a herd of cattle, horses, and mules, and harvested crops from his farm near the community of Thackerville, located in a loop of the Red River about ten miles south of the modern town of Marietta. In 1882, a year before the birth of his son, Frank Criner Love, Robert and the family moved to a ranch located about twelve miles south of the South Canadian River.

Robert became a community leader in the northern section of the Chickasaw Nation with solid assets and growing ambitions. His big break came in 1885 when Congress authorized the construction of the second railroad through the Indian Territory, a line that would become known as the Santa Fe. After survey crews marked the north-south route of the line, construction crews cleared the right-of-way and started building bridges and laying tracks from Gainesville, Texas,

PURCELL, I.T.   1889.

north across the Red River toward a spot on the South Canadian River where they would meet crews laying tracks from the north. Robert, representing a third generation of Chickasaw entrepreneurs, won a contract to provide fresh meat to feed the construction gangs along this early day interstate transportation corridor.

In March of 1887, as crews approached the village of Pauls Valley, two merchants from Silver City jumped ahead of the moving tent town and built a fourteen-by-twenty-foot store and a dug-out cellar along the south bank of the South Canadian River where a bridge was to be built. Robert Love built a slaughter pen about a half mile east of the store and moved a herd of cattle to the surrounding grasslands so he could furnish beef to the hungry workers.

On April 5, 1887, about two weeks before construction crews drove the last spike completing the Santa Fe line north and south across the territory, Love exercised his right as a Chickasaw citizen to claim the land surrounding the depot. With a partner handling a team of horses, Robert grabbed a turning plow and marked off two streets. One was called Main Street. The other was Chickasaw Avenue. He sold his first lots later that day and made an offer to any Chickasaw citizen willing to move to the new town. They could have two free lots, one for a business and another for a home.

The frontier community grew slowly. The first building was a sixteen-by-thirty-foot log building posing as a hotel, followed by a

The town of Purcell was founded by Tom Love's great-grandfather, Robert J. Love, on the Santa Fe rail line that crossed the Chickasaw Nation in 1887.

The Land Run of April 22, 1889, lured more than 50,000 pioneers to the lands directly north of the Chickasaw Nation, creating opportunities for Love family enterprises.

Despite the slow start, Robert's town-building venture was timed perfectly to take advantage of the first land run.

Above: Travelers moving through the Indian Territory by railroad offered another opportunity for Robert J. Love, who built the Love Hotel in Purcell.

Facing page: By 1901 and the opening of the Kiowa and Comanche lands to non-Indian settlers by lottery, the economic boom on the Southern Great Plains was just beginning. Population growth and the countdown to statehood encouraged the Love family to invest in banks and cotton.

post office established on April 21, 1887, and a newspaper called the *Purcell Register* that released its first edition in November of that same year. On the eve of the land run into the Unassigned Lands on April 22, 1889, the resident population of Purcell grew to approximately 200 people while the transient community of those gathering for the run grew by thousands.

Despite the slow start, Robert's town-building venture was timed perfectly to take advantage of the first land run. To the north, across the nearby South Canadian River, thousands of homesteading families who had claimed 160-acre farms too late in the season to grow a crop needed supplies and tools. During that first winter of rabbit meat and turnips, Purcell served as a staging point for relief shipments moving north out of the Chickasaw Nation and the state of Texas. When the first crops did come in north of the river, Purcell was the gateway for shipments moving south along the steel tracks of the Santa Fe.

Robert took advantage of the growing opportunities offered by timing and location. He founded the Chickasaw Bank, which eventually merged with the Bank of Purcell and became the Chickasaw National Bank. In 1897, as rains returned to the Southern Plains and farmers harvested bumper crops of cotton, Robert and his partners built the Purcell Cotton Seed Oil Company mill. His most famous investment, however, was the Love Hotel.

In 1895, following three fires that destroyed much of the downtown business district of Purcell, Robert invested $20,000 in a sixty-three-room, three-story brick hotel that one correspondent called "the finest hotel in the Chickasaw Nation that has but one equal in the territory." The Love Hotel featured electric lights, steam heat, a dining room, sample rooms for salesmen, and a barber shop. Seven decades before his great grandson would launch his own business catering to people moving from one place to another, Robert Love served travelers along the interstate transportation highway of his generation.

In 1899, just as his investments in the Love Hotel, the Chickasaw National Bank, and the Purcell Cotton Seed Oil Company were beginning to pay off with the booming economy, Robert J. Love died at the young age of forty-seven. Fortunately for his wife, Sallie, he left behind not only assets in bricks and mortar but also ten children to carry on the family businesses. One of those children, only sixteen years old at the time of his father's death, would rise to the challenge.

His name was Frank Criner Love, the grandfather of Tom Love.

A Group of Typical Land-Seekers

They are of all ages and nationalities, and many applications have been filed by women, who stood in line with the others for hours at a time

Fort Sill, the Government Post

In the heart of the new country. Seventy acres surrounding the post are reserved Fort Sill is destined to become one of the most important in the section

The Canadian River—Boundary of the New Country

Which is well watered, and likely to be very productive

Scott Mountain, of the Wichita Range

This is in the midst of the new territory

Settlers Awaiting the Signal at the previous Opening of Territory

THE LAST RUSH FOR HOMES IN OKLAHOMA

Many thousand applications for homesteads have been filed for the drawing which is to take place August 6. On previous occasions it has been the custom to range the would-be settlers in line, and then, at a pistol-shot, each would make at top speed for the site selected. This year the affair is managed differently, the owners for the sites being selected in somewhat the same manner as prizes are drawn for in a lottery

Frank, born in 1883, lived at a time when the world around him was rapidly changing. Politically, his tribe was under assault from a federal government that was determined to destroy the Indian nations and integrate Chickasaws and other Indian people into the mainstream of American life. In 1898, Congress passed the Curtis Act, which disbanded tribal courts, accelerated the allotment of all communally-owned lands to individual Indians, and set the clock ticking for statehood. Frank, along with other members of his family, received an allotment of 320 acres but lost his tribal government. There is no record of what he thought about the proposed but rejected Indian state of Sequoyah, the naming of a county after the Love family, or the ultimate admission of Oklahoma to the Union as the 46th state on November 16, 1907.

The pain of losing his tribal government may have been cushioned somewhat by the economic boom in Oklahoma from 1898 to 1929. The foundation of the boom was agriculture, which prospered with new land openings, high prices for cotton and wheat, and a growing network of railroads that provided a way to get crops and livestock to distant markets and manufactured goods to pioneers who wanted homes, schools, and consumer goods. Purcell, located at the junction of the north-to-south Santa Fe Railroad and the east-to-west Oklahoma Central Railway, became a hub for the trans-shipment of cotton, wheat, corn, hogs, and cattle.

Oil added fuel to the regional economic boom. The first commercially successful oil well in Oklahoma was drilled near Bartlesville in 1898 and the first giant field called Glennpool was discovered southwest of Tulsa in 1905. For the next twenty-five years wildcatters opened a succession of new fields such as the Greater Osage, Three Sands, Healdton, Cushing, Seminole, and the biggest of them all, Oklahoma City, which was discovered in December of 1928. Rising from the early oil patch in Oklahoma came homegrown companies such as Phillips, Conoco, Skelly, Sunray DX, Champlin, Apco, and Sinclair.

The combination of agricultural prosperity and oil production made Oklahoma the fastest growing state in the Union from 1910 to 1930. Oklahoma City grew more than 640 percent in one decade; Tulsa became the Oil Capital of the World; and towns such as Purcell grew with jobs and investments linked to other communities by a network of steel rails and an emerging highway system launched on a statewide basis in 1923. For frontier entrepreneurs such as Frank Criner Love, Oklahoma was the land of opportunity in the first decades of the 20th century.

For frontier entrepreneurs such as Frank Criner Love, Oklahoma was the land of opportunity in the first decades of the 20th century.

Tom Love's father, Frank Criner Love II, did not follow his father and grandfather in the banking business. Instead, he found opportunity in the worlds of law and the energy industry.

When his father died in 1899, Frank was enrolled at the Wentworth Military Academy in Missouri, where he excelled in the emerging rough and tumble sport of football. He returned to Purcell and his family, opened a real estate and insurance business, and married Louamma Edwards, the daughter of a dentist in Gainesville, Texas. She had come to Purcell as a school teacher. After they married in 1905, they spent their first year in the easy comfort of the Love Hotel.

In 1908, a year after statehood, their first child was born, a son they named Frank Criner, Jr., which later was shortened to F.C. In his hometown he was known as "Boots." The elder Frank shared his passion for hunting and fishing with his son, and together, they spent as much time as possible riding horses and working cattle on their 320-acre Chickasaw allotment near Maysville, Oklahoma. Soon, the family expanded with the birth of a daughter, Sally, also called "Pansy," and twin girls, Pauline and Shirley, better known as "Polly" and "Peggy."

By 1920, Frank Sr. was president of the Chickasaw National Bank. He invested in real estate, including a stately two-story brick home on double lots that included a clay tennis court. The house was big enough to host F.C.'s senior prom. After graduating from Purcell High School, F.C. attended the University of Oklahoma, which was located across the river a few miles to the north. There, he joined a fraternity, rose to the rank of colonel in the R.O.T.C., and entered the law school. In 1929, the tall, red-headed "big man on campus" noticed a beautiful young girl during pledge week. One day, while she was walking past a miniature golf course, he took her arm in stride and told her he had been trying to get a date with her for weeks. Soon she was wearing his pin. The young lady who would be his partner for the rest of his life was Margaret Vessels.

Margaret had been raised in Enid, where her father was a prominent banker and community leader. She was surrounded by family, including her mother and father, four brothers, one sister, and a grandmother and aunt who lived next door. She attended St. Joseph's parochial school through grade eight, then Enid High School where she was editor of the school newspaper. Her favorite topics in school were French and elocution.

Near the end of her second year at college, Margaret's world of comfort and romance was shaken when her father lost his bank in the growing shadows of the Great Depression. When the semester ended, her father abruptly moved the entire family to Brownsville, Texas, where he sold real estate, peddled goods door-to-door, and traded oil leases. Making the best of the hard times, Margaret

Above: Margaret Vessels, raised in Enid, met young F.C. Love when they were enrolled at the University of Oklahoma.

...as Margaret would later write, "he [F.C.] was incapable of an ungenerous, dishonest action or even thought."

Facing page: F.C. and Margaret Love continued the family tradition of community service. F.C. complemented his leadership at Kerr-McGee with service as a reform candidate on the city council and inner-city redevelopment during the early stages of urban renewal.

Dean McGee (left) and Robert S. Kerr combined their talents to create one of the most diversified energy and chemical companies in the country in the 1940s and 1950s. Just as they were starting to expand, they recruited a promising young attorney, F.C. Love, who would eventually serve the company as president.

From the 1940s to the 1960s, F.C.'s career matched the meteoric rise of Kerr-McGee from a regional contract drilling firm to a fully integrated energy and chemical giant on the world stage.

approached the local newspaper and proposed a weekly column called "Shopping with Sue." For a few dollars paid by the line, she wrote about products that could be found in local stores—as long as they bought advertising in the newspaper. She also wrote a steady series of letters to F.C. Love. As she would later write, "he was incapable of an ungenerous, dishonest action or even thought." She was in love and they became engaged during her exile in Texas.

In the meantime, tragedy struck F.C.'s family when his father, only forty-seven-years-old, died suddenly from a a heart attack. His mother, Louamma, and the twin girls moved to Norman to be near F.C. and Sally, but returned to Purcell the next year. She sold the big house, built a smaller home where the tennis court had been, and found a way to support the twins first as a tag agent and then as the co-owner of an insurance agency. She also managed the family farm, which would remain a meager but important source of income throughout the Great Depression.

With his family secure in Purcell, F.C. graduated from law school and found a job in Oklahoma City paying $50 a month. He borrowed his mother's Ford coupe and drove to Brownsville, Texas. On December 29, 1931, F.C. and Margaret were married in a simple ceremony. Two children quickly followed, one a son named Frank Criner Love III and the other a daughter named Sally. Shortly after her birth, F.C. was offered a job in Tulsa with Shell Oil Company at a salary of $250 a month. They lived in the Oil Capital of the World for the next year.

In 1937, despite a national recession prolonging the hard times of the Great Depression, F.C. moved back to Oklahoma City to join the law firm of Embry, Johnson, Crowe and Tolbert, the successor to the modern-day firm of Crowe and Dunlevy. At first the little family moved into a rented home at 17th Street and N. Robinson Avenue, but with the birth of another baby they bought a home at 2124 N.W. 20th Street, not far from Rosary Catholic Church. They named their third child Thomas, quickly shortened to Tom.

As the Love family grew to seven children with the births of Kathy, Charles, Margaret, and Jack, F.C.'s business career reflected the improving economy. He won a lawsuit filed by a lease holder against an oil company based in Oklahoma City. Then he represented that company in a lawsuit after casing in an oil well collapsed and dumped mud and water into the Wilcox sand. When the production of surrounding wells decreased, the owners sued F.C.'s client for millions of dollars, which would have ruined the fledgling start-up. In 1946, after years of testimony and legal filings, F.C. won the case. His client was the recently renamed Kerr-McGee Oil Industries, Inc.

Robert S. Kerr, the former governor of Oklahoma and a first-term United States Senator who had founded Kerr-McGee, asked F.C. to come to his office after the victory. He offered the young attorney a job and asked what salary he needed to leave the law firm. F.C. said $25,000 a year. Kerr responded by offering $30,000 a year plus stock options. In October of 1947, F.C. Love became executive vice president and assistant to the chief operating officer, Dean A. McGee.

From the 1940s to the 1960s, F.C.'s career matched the meteoric rise of Kerr-McGee from a regional contract drilling firm to a fully integrated energy and chemical giant on the world stage. According to one historian, F.C. was an indispensable asset to the company in a volatile industry that demanded a delicate balancing act between crisis management and calculated risk. He wrote, "F.C. was a naturally cautious, six-feet-tall, easy-to-blush, warm-hearted diplomat with a talent for negotiation and the skills of a careful student in all activities." His legal and personal skills were a good

Tom Love (standing in center) was the third-born child in the close-knit family raised by F.C. and Margaret Love.

From 1910 to the 1920s, refineries were built across Oklahoma as oil fields were discovered. Kerr-McGee would eventually operate two refineries to supply a growing chain of service stations.

When Tom and Judy married in 1960, Oklahoma City and the state were at an economic crossroads. The twin booms of oil and agriculture had peaked and the new era of industrialization and diversification were just getting started. Although traumatic for some, the change created opportunity for many.

match for Kerr's aggressive vision built on expansion and McGee's knowledge of geology and exploration. Together, they would need all their combined skills in the coming decades.

The shift from drilling contractor with a small refinery in Wynnewood to a vertically integrated energy company began with a challenging crisis in 1951 when Tom was fourteen years old. The domestic land-based drilling industry was stagnant, with cheap imported oil dragging the price of oil below the cost of exploration and production in Oklahoma. Meanwhile, the embryonic off-shore search for oil in the Gulf of Mexico came to a sudden halt following a U.S. Supreme Court ruling that disputed whether the states or the federal government controlled leasing in the Gulf. At the time, Kerr-McGee had twenty-six drilling rigs and ten of those were stacked for lack of demand.

Company leaders launched an aggressive effort to diversify in the crosswinds of that uncertain future. To complement aggressive expansion into off-shore drilling technology, they created a

research division that could use science to add value to oil-based products such as pipeline wrap, plastic cements, paint bases, roofing felts, and waterproofing compounds. In 1952, they diverted even more dramatically from their past by creating the Navajo Uranium Company and a company to mine potash needed for the fertilizer industry. Other industrial ventures launched during this five-year diversification effort included the production of helium, asphalt, and lubricants.

As F.C. moved up the chain of command to company treasurer and executive vice president in charge of operations, Kerr-McGee boldly moved into the retail distribution of gasoline and diesel fuel. In 1955, they bought Deep Rock Oil Company, based in Cushing, Oklahoma, that included a refinery, a pipeline network, and 800 service stations across the Southwest. A year later, F.C. negotiated the purchase of Knox Industries, based in Enid, with another 225 service stations. That was followed by the acquisition of Triangle Refineries of Houston, Texas, with eleven oil terminals and a fleet of barges, tank cars, and tankers to move more than 20 million barrels of oil a year.

Within one decade of aggressive expansion, Kerr-McGee owned an integrated network of companies that drilled for and produced oil, refined it into marketable products, transported it from place to place, and sold the refined products to retail customers with more than 1,700 service stations. According to one company insider, "McGee provided the driving force, while Love handled the possibility of trouble and unforeseen opportunity." In recognition of his trail of success, F.C. Love was named president of Kerr-McGee in 1967.

By the time he retired six years later, Kerr-McGee was the twentieth largest oil company in the United States.

Although unaware of it at the time, young Tom Love one day would gladly embrace the entrepreneurial spirit of his extended family dating back five generations. Until that day arrived, however, Tom was more concerned about life at home, fun in the neighborhood, and keeping up at school.

Tom was an infant when the family moved to the house at 2124 N.W. 20th Street. It was a two-story, three-bedroom home built in the 1930s as Oklahoma City stretched to the end of the streetcar lines west of Pennsylvania Avenue. His world was measured by the distance he and his friends could walk. They fished in Shepherd Lake, located

By the 1950s, competition was intense in the retail sector of gasoline sales. Some service stations were affiliated with major oil companies, while most were run by independent operators.

In recognition of his trail of success, F.C. Love was named president of Kerr-McGee in 1967.

on an undeveloped 160-acre homestead where Shepherd Mall later would be built. They walked to neighborhood movie theaters such as the Plaza on 16th Street, the Tower on 23rd Street, and the May on May Avenue. They walked two blocks to the parochial school at Rosary Catholic Church where Dominican nuns dressed in full habits pushed their young wards. Years later, Tom would remember the nuns as "tough," but he quickly added, "they had to be."

To Tom, his father was a towering figure, a little distant, who seemed to always be at work, whereas his mother and siblings were memorable parts of his daily life. Frank was five years older, a brilliant student, with a talent for writing. Sally, three years older, was "miss perfect" in the eyes of her younger brother. She played the piano, sang beautifully, and excelled at school. Their mother, devoted to her husband and his career, spent much of her time taking care of the home, raising the four younger siblings, and impressing everyone who knew her. Family vacations typically were to Colorado. In a car full of kids and luggage, they started each summer trek headed west on Route 66.

By the time he was fourteen years old, Tom was working part time as a roustabout cutting weeds and doing odd jobs on summer break around Kerr-McGee and Deep Rock pipe yards on the south side of Oklahoma City. He spent another summer doing odd jobs around a refinery. When he turned sixteen, he drove his '49 Chevy to the Texas Panhandle where he got a job at a Kerr-McGee divisional office near the oil town of Sunray. Years later, Tom would remember a lesson learned about responsibility during that first summer away from home.

He was working as a swamper, which meant he did anything needed at the moment, for a company man named Fibber McGee. They had taken a truck to Dumas to pick up a load of drill stem pipe when Tom convinced the older man that he could drive the truck back to the well site, even though he was barely sixteen years old and did not have a commercial driver's license. Tom was a big kid with plenty of affable confidence, so Fibber gave him the wheel. As they were barreling down the road at sixty miles per hour, a driver in another truck suddenly turned in front of them. Tom had no time to react and the two trucks collided. Miraculously, no one was hurt.

Harry Limes, Kerr-McGee's division director, came to the site and told Tom to tell the highway patrolman exactly what had happened. Tom did as instructed. When they got back to the office, Harry talked first to Fibber and then asked Tom to come in. "I should fire Fibber for letting you drive that truck," he said, "but I am not going to do it because he is a good guy with a family to support." Then Harry made a point that Tom would never forget. "You are old enough to take responsibility for your actions, and you talked Fibber into letting you drive. It almost cost you your life and it almost cost him his job. You did not cause the wreck, but you made a mistake. Next time, think before you act."

Lessons in responsibility, coupled with ethics, discipline, and hard work became part of Tom's daily routine in 1951 when his parents enrolled him at St. Gregory's College preparatory school, an all-boys boarding school located about thirty miles east of Oklahoma City near the town of Shawnee. The history of the school dated to 1875, when a group of Benedictine monks founded Sacred Heart Mission near Atoka in the Choctaw Nation. In 1910, the abbey and school were moved to Shawnee, where the monks built Benedictine Hall to house the church, administrative offices, a library, and most of the classes. The five-story brick building opened in 1915 with a class of forty students.

The curriculum, like the daily regimen, was structured and demanding when Tom arrived as a freshman. Each day started with Mass, followed by breakfast, classes, lunch, more classes, sports, dinner, and two hours of study hall in the evening before lights out. Tom had four years of Latin, worked on the student newspaper staff for two years, and served as a class officer for three years, including class secretary-treasurer his junior year and class president his senior year. During his sophomore year, Tom had a growth spurt and became a lineman on the football team his junior and senior years. By the time he graduated in the spring of 1955, he was six-feet, three-inches tall and weighed more than 200 pounds. His team finished the season with a record of eight wins and two losses.

Almost sixty years later, Tom would remember his life at St. Gregory's as a "character forming experience." He was inspired by the service of the Benedictines, who were universally well educated, and was pushed by the demanding curriculum and structure of the school. It was close enough to home to be with his family during holidays and over the summer, but distant enough to create a bond with his fellow classmates that would last a lifetime. "It was not for everybody," Tom later recalled, "but it was perfect for me." He graduated in a class of fifty seniors in 1955.

As a lineman and tight end, Tom received an invitation to play football at St. John's University, a Catholic college in rural Minnesota where future Hall of Fame coach John Gagliardi had just taken over the football team in 1953. Gagliardi would remain at the school for sixty-three years and win four NCAA Division III national championships and 464 victories, the most in NCAA

Benedictine Hall on the campus of St. Gregory's College preparatory school in Shawnee was the center of Tom Love's life for four years when he was teenager. The lessons learned would serve him well as both a businessman and community leader.

After one year in college, Tom joined the Marines and served with distinction.

history. Tom Love, one of his promising freshman players, enjoyed the experience but did not make the grades expected by his father. After one year in college, Tom did not return to school.

Tom was soon distracted by two events that would help shape his life. One was a letter from his local draft board, but instead of waiting to be drafted into the Army, Tom joined four of his friends and enlisted in the Marine Corps buddy program. Joining him were Duane Evans, Johnny Zehrung, and Dan Holman, all classmates at St. Gregory's, and Mike Keefe, who had attended Catholic High School, later renamed after Bishop McGuinness. The other distraction was a girl he had met while home during the Easter break. Her name was Judy McCarthy.

Judy McCarthy met and dated Tom before he joined the Marines. While he served his country, she attended college at the University of Oklahoma.

Born in Chicago, Illinois, Judy had moved to Oklahoma City in 1942 when her father landed a job as district manager and salesman in the local office of a national outdoor advertising company. The family consisted of her mother, Ruth, her father, Ed, two brothers, and two sisters. They bought a house in Crown Heights and the children attended John Carroll School and Catholic High School, where Judy excelled in journalism and drama. Over the Easter holiday of 1956, while enrolled at Oklahoma State University as a journalism major, she met Tom Love through mutual friends. Their blind date was an evening at the Cedar Terrace Club, a dance hall located on Wilshire Avenue on the far north side of Oklahoma City.

When Tom returned home in May after the end of his freshman year at St. John's, he called Judy and asked for another date, then another. By the time he reported for induction into the Marine Corps, they were going steady and parted promising to write one another. In July of 1956, that parting came quickly when Tom and his buddies boarded an airplane bound for San Diego, California, and basic training.

Their drill instructor was Sergeant Sorrenson, a long, lean, battle-tested soldier who had joined the Army at the age of fifteen. After fighting in Korea, he was mustered out when his age was discovered, but later joined the Marines when he reached legal age. Of the seventy members in the platoon, more than a dozen washed out before basic was completed four months later.

After basic training, Tom was assigned to a test command developing amphibious tracked vehicles at 29 Palms near Barstow, California, which included actual beach landings in the rough

Judy (standing on the left) grew up in a house in Crown Heights with two brothers, two sisters, and her parents, Ed and Ruth McCarthy.

waters of the Pacific Ocean. He injured his back during one training exercise and would suffer the consequences the rest of his life. Tom, who was 235 pounds of bone and muscle under the demanding training, would vividly remember the challenges more than fifty years later. "I would not give a million dollars for that experience," he said.

While Tom was learning to be a Marine, Judy enrolled at the University of Oklahoma, where she majored in journalism. Her main interest, however, was Tom Love. They exchanged a steady stream of letters and saw each other during his short furloughs home. In May of 1957, accompanied by her mother, Judy traveled to San Diego and spent a week with him. By the time Tom returned home after two years of active duty, Judy had dropped out of school at the end of her sophomore year.

Tom and Judy dated for another two and a half years. He enrolled in college, first at the University of Oklahoma and then at Central State College, later renamed the University of Central

Tom and Judy were married the day after Christmas in 1960. With a limited budget, Judy took advantage of a church already decorated with flowers for the holiday.

By the time Tom and Judy decided to launch their first full-service gasoline station, they had two children, Greg (middle) and Laura (right). At the time Judy was expecting their third child, Jennifer (left).

Oklahoma. She found a job working in the mailroom at the Sohio Oil Company. To improve her employment skills she enrolled at the Draughn's School of Business to study typing and short hand, which led to a job opening at Pan American Oil Company. Although she failed the stenographer's test, she called them repeatedly and finally got a job working for a middle manager.

After almost five years of courtship, Tom and Judy were married on December 26, 1960. The date was carefully chosen to stretch their meager wedding budget of $300. On the day after Christmas, the church was already decorated with flowers. The newlyweds moved into a small rental house near N.W. 19th Street and Portland Avenue, less than a mile from where Tom had grown up as a teenager. Their first child, Gregory Michael Love, was born ten months and ten days later. Shortly thereafter, they bought their first home at 1713 Westchester Drive on the north side of Oklahoma City. The three-bedroom, 1,100-square-foot house purchased at a cost of $11,000 was soon filled with another child, a daughter they named Laura Anne Love.

In the summer of 1963, with a wife, two babies, and a home mortgage, Tom took a job as a service station trainee with Kerr-

Tom thought he could develop a business model that would have one primary selling point—the cheapest gas in town.

McGee. He was assigned to the training station at N.W. 36th Street and Santa Fe Avenue, where a man named Charlie Drake taught recruits the fundamentals of the business. With experience growing up around the oil and gas business, Tom learned quickly and managed the station for a month.

Tom's purpose in joining the training program, however, did not include working an eight-hour shift filling gas tanks and cleaning windshields. His goal was to learn more about the business of buying and selling gasoline, an idea he had been nurturing for a while as he came to the conclusion that college was not going to get him where he wanted to go. If he could find an abandoned filling station in a small town, lease it on liberal terms with no money down, he thought he could develop a business model that would have one primary selling point—the cheapest gas in town. In January of 1964, to test his theory, Tom leased an abandoned filling station in Watonga, Oklahoma.

Tom and Judy would never look back.

THE CHEAPEST GAS IN TOWN

2

The willingness to take a risk and start a business requires a combination of confidence and ambition. In the winter of 1963, Tom and Judy Love had both in abundance, thanks to a legacy of family influence and personal experience. Those assets, however, were mixed with one other factor driving them forward. They had few options.

Tom had decided against pursuing his college degree, so any professional

Tom Love decided to get into the retail gasoline business at a time of transition in the way service stations were managed and branded. He found a niche on the edges of the industry.

career would start at the entry level and require years of climbing a company ladder. They had no savings to invest and no property to serve as collateral for a loan, so any business opportunity would have to be built on hard work and ingenuity alone. They needed an opportunity, a niche somewhere in the marketplace that fit their talents and Tom's knowledge of the oil and gas industry where he had experience working summers and vacations around pipe yards, pump jacks, and refineries.

Tom thought he saw that opportunity on the fringe of retail gasoline sales. With no assets, he knew he needed to avoid big cities where real estate was expensive and major oil companies and long

---

Not surprisingly, Tom looked west, the same direction his Chickasaw ancestors had fled more than a century earlier...

established jobbers dominated the
marketplace. He needed a good
location in a small town, a market
where the competition was soft
and customers would come from
a combination of local residents
and travelers. The next question
was where.

Not surprisingly, Tom looked
west, the same direction his
Chickasaw ancestors had fled
more than a century earlier, the
same direction Dust Bowl migrants
had sought hope for a new life, and
the same direction that symbolized
the American dream. For Tom
and Judy Love, that dream led
to Watonga, Oklahoma, and a
retail gasoline industry that was
on the threshold of major changes.

Opportunities in the world of retail gasoline sales had long been linked to the overlapping progress of cars, trucks, highway construction, and the oil industry. It started with the first successful American car assembled in 1893 by Charles and Frank Duryea, two bicycle mechanics in Springfield, Massachusetts. By 1907, the same year Oklahoma gained statehood, American manufacturers produced more than 44,000 cars a year while William Durant was already running General Motors and Henry Ford was promoting a versatile little "runabout" called the Model T. With the efficiency of mass production and the construction of assembly plants across the country in places like Oklahoma City, the price of a new car plunged to $400 by 1915.

World War I and industrial expansion in the 1920s added a new chapter to this transportation revolution. While credit on the installment plan made cars accessible to farmers and middle class families, trucks posed a new challenge to railroads as a cheaper and more flexible means of moving goods and people from one point to another. In Oklahoma, a local farm boy named Whit Lee started a bus line from Clinton to Oklahoma City in 1931 and grew his business into an interstate trucking giant called LeeWay Freight Lines.

Reliance on cars and trucks led to a growing public demand for more and better roads. When Oklahoma became a state, the primary responsibility for building and maintaining roads was

Demand for gasoline increased in tandem with the popularity and affordability of cars. In 1915, Henry Ford was leading the industry to record production when he built this Model T assembly plant in Oklahoma City.

given to city officials and county commissioners with only slight assistance from either the state or federal governments. Not surprisingly, the emerging system of improved roads was not coordinated very well and the few paved roads typically stopped at municipal and county lines.

Congress responded by passing the Federal Highway Act of 1921, which provided fifty-fifty matching grants to the states for the construction of paved roads. Oklahoma responded by creating the modern Oklahoma Highway Commission in 1923 with a true statewide network of roads and the first state tax on the sale of gasoline to provide the match for federal road funds. A good example of early success was Route 66, started in 1925 and completely paved from Chicago to Los Angeles by 1937. The man responsible for coordinating that first interstate highway system and the father of Route 66 was Cyrus Avery, a county commissioner from Tulsa, Oklahoma.

The rising use of trucks and automobiles in turn created a growing demand for gasoline and diesel fuel, which were made from oil. And with growing demand for oil came a growing supply from the old oil region of Pennsylvania, West Virginia, and Southern Ohio and the new oil states of Texas, California, and Oklahoma. Wildcatters such as J. Paul Getty, Harry Sinclair, Frank Phillips, and E.W. Marland discovered a succession of oil fields that ranged from the beaches of Southern California to the hills of Oklahoma. Along with the derricks and pump jacks came refineries

Reliance on cars and trucks led to a growing public demand for more and better roads.

With more cars and trucks came more miles of paved highways. In Oklahoma, the great leap forward came in 1923 when the first motor fuel tax was levied on the sale of gasoline to provide matching funds for federal grants. Two years later, Route 66 was being paved through the state.

that used heat to "crack" the complex carbon molecules of oil into marketable products such as gasoline, diesel, asphalt, and lubricating grease. By World War II, Oklahoma alone had twenty-two refineries scattered across the state, including one in Tulsa that covered more than a square mile.

Major oil companies and wholesale merchants called jobbers delivered the products coming out of refineries to the drivers of cars and trucks at retail outlets called service stations. Jobbers bought gasoline and diesel at the refinery gate or at terminals built

CUSHING REFINERY ~ CUSHING. OKLA.

Refineries were built throughout Oklahoma as a succession of giant oil fields were discovered. Tulsa, with one refinery that covered a square mile, became the Oil Capital of the World. Cushing, where this Sinclair Refinery was built after 1912, became the pipeline nexus of the nation.

along a network of pipelines, and hauled the bulk product either to their own service stations or sold it to other dealers. A good example of an early jobber is the family of Barney Brown, Jr.

In 1937, Barney Brown, Sr. opened his first service station at S.W. 10th and Walker in Oklahoma City. With the help of his two sons, their little company expanded into wholesale distribution of gasoline and opened a new, expanded operation in Stockyards City that included space for their trucks, a service station, wash bay, grocery store, and restaurant. In 1957, as major oil companies started opening their own branded stations, Barney Jr. bought Red Rock distributors, the first Conoco jobber in the state, and expanded with his own chain of Texaco and Apco service stations and an early version of a truck stop near the southern end of the Turner Turnpike.

His competitors operated under brands such as Conoco, Phillips 66, Champlin, Texaco, Skelly, Mobil, Sunray DX, Knox, Apco, and Deep Rock. In some cases, the service stations were owned by oil companies but managed by independent operators who received a combination of contracted salary and a commission based on sales and services. Other stations were owned by local investors who leased the facilities to the oil companies. Prior to the early 1970s the supply of gasoline far outstripped demand, so the key factors for success or failure became location, price, and the quality of full service.

Full service took many forms. In most cases, it included washing the windshield, checking the oil, and airing the tires, which could result in the sale of wiper blades, oil, or tires. Additional services might include light mechanical repairs, car washing, and the use of credit cards, green stamps, or free gifts. One notable premium offered by Knox service station dealers was a set of frosted ice tea glasses and matching pitcher featuring paintings by the famous Indian artist, Acee Blue Eagle. With each fill-up, a customer would get another glass in the set.

Tom Love, while working summers and vacations, saw Kerr-McGee ease into the full service gasoline business, even if it was through the back door. The transition began in 1945 when Robert S. Kerr convinced his board of directors to buy a small refinery in Wynnewood, a small town located about forty miles south of Oklahoma City where he wanted to produce asphalt for the growing highway construction industry. The aging plant was bought from the family of Josh Cosden for $250,000, and after three years and several upgrades, the annual profit exceeded the cost of acquisition.

Dean McGee, who still preferred exploration and production as the core business of the company, concluded that they had to either get all in or all out of the refinery business. There was no "in between" because the most competitive, lowest price margin at any stage of the petroleum business was at the refinery gate. To add value, they had to go into retail sales, and if they were going to operate service stations, they needed more refining capacity.

In 1955, Kerr-McGee purchased Deep Rock, which included a refinery in Cushing, 347,260 net acres of undeveloped leases, a pipeline system, 575 employees, and more than 800 distributors selling gasoline under the Deep Rock brand. The next year, Kerr-McGee acquired Knox Oil Company, which included a small refinery, gathering pipelines, and a string of retail service stations.

The Knox Oil Company, founded in Enid, Oklahoma, built a chain of service stations where they offered premiums such as these frosted serving glasses with images by Acee Blue Eagle, a famous Oklahoma Indian artist.

As late as the 1960s, a combination of cheap imported oil and intense competition between service stations kept retail gasoline prices below thirty cents a gallon.

By 1959, with a goal of adding seventy-five new service stations a year, Kerr-McGee had more than 1,200 branded outlets, a system-wide credit card, and a training program designed to promote what they called "high quality driveway service."

By the time Tom and Judy were married in 1960, Kerr-McGee and most of the major oil companies were already upgrading and concentrating their branded service stations where they could justify the costs of bigger buildings and advertising on television. Typically, the majors increasingly focused on urban markets and the emerging network of interstate highways launched during the administration of President Dwight D. Eisenhower. Kerr-McGee invested heavily in a string of new stations stretching west to Arizona along Interstate Highway 40. In Oklahoma City, where Kerr-McGee had seventeen branded stations by 1965, a recurring television commercial featured a beautiful female model in evening wear holding a can of Blue Velvet Motor Oil.

As major brands shifted to urban and interstate locations in the late 1950s and early 1960s, they abandoned marginal stations in small towns dotted across the map. In most cases, the major oil companies lost nothing other than volume sales because the stations were usually owned by local businessmen who had leased the property to them under multi-year contracts. Once the contracts expired, the majors moved on and the local owners had a piece of property that was paid for but earning nothing while empty. What they needed was a hungry operator to lease the property and generate at least a trickle of revenue.

That was the opportunity that Tom and Judy Love were looking for in the winter of 1963.

Soon after opening his first service station, Tom joined the Oklahoma Jobbers Council, a trade group representing the interests of those in the business of distributing and selling gasoline.

Tom had an idea. He knew he could purchase gasoline at one of many refineries around the state and have ten days to pay the bill, which was the industry standard. If he could sell the gasoline within those ten days and cover overhead costs, he could pay the refinery and order another load. In effect, the refinery would "loan" him his start-up inventory and carry him on a cash account. For an entrepreneur with no capital to invest and no balance sheet to borrow money, it was Tom's only chance of getting started.

The next step was finding an abandoned service station that would require no investment up front and be in the right location to get both local customers and the traveling public. Looking west, Tom narrowed his focus on Watonga, located about sixty miles west

Judy kept the books for the fledgling company for the first few years, using a roll top desk in their family home. She and Tom are seen here with son Greg and daughter Laura.

of Oklahoma City. The town was the right size, with a population hovering around 4,000, and a mixed economy that included farming and ranching, marginal oil production, and light industry. In 1963, the town had a cheese factory, a nearby gypsum wallboard plant, three schools, eight churches, three grain elevators, and a commercial district with a C.R. Anthony's clothing store, a T.G.&Y. Variety Store, and two grocery stores. The local population would provide a solid pool of repeat customers.

Watonga's appeal as a location for Tom's first service station was enhanced by the fact that it was at the crossroads of State Highway 8, which ran north and south, and U.S. Highway 270/State Highway 3, which was the main diagonal route that ran southeast to northwest from Oklahoma City to the Oklahoma Panhandle on the

Tom's first service station after filing articles of incorporation as Musket Corporation (facing page), was located in Watonga (above and right). It was branded as a Knox station with gasoline purchased from a Kerr-McGee refinery.

way to New Mexico and Colorado. Additional customers passing through that intersection during summers and holidays would be tourists bound for nearby Roman Nose State Park, one of the first seven state parks established in Oklahoma in 1937.

Tom found his abandoned service station at 304 West C Street, two blocks off the main commercial district and two blocks from the intersection of the two highways. The building was owned by Calvin Pierce, a local businessman who had built the stucco structure in the 1950s as a branded Mobil station. Most recently, it had operated as an independent service station under the name of Save-More. Although the pumps were gone, it had everything Tom needed to sell gasoline, including two underground tanks, one for regular and one for ethyl, an office, and two bays, one for washing cars and the other outfitted with a power lift for light mechanical work. Most importantly, the price was right. Tom and Judy signed a lease that was less than $150 a month.

With high hopes, the budding entrepreneurs thought they needed to incorporate their little company with the State of Oklahoma. They called Jerry Sokolosky, one of Tom's good friends from high school, who agreed to file the papers at no charge. Then he asked for the formal name to be filed. Tom and Judy looked at each other, told him they would get back to him the next day, and spent part of that evening going through an old dictionary. When they came to the word "musket," it struck them as simple yet masculine. On January 16, 1964, papers were filed creating the Musket Corporation.

The next challenge was finding a steady supply of gasoline. Like many independent jobbers, Tom wanted to rely as much as possible on spot purchases because the price at the "back gate" of a refinery was always cheaper. The down side was the unpredictability of when a refinery would sell "distressed" gasoline just to move it out of inventory to make room for more production. To hedge that bet, Tom made a deal with Kerr-McGee to secure gasoline from their refineries. For every two independent service stations Tom brought to Kerr-McGee, they would not only guarantee a steady supply of gasoline, but they also would lease him one of their abandoned stations in a small town.

With a source for gasoline and a building under lease, Tom thought he needed only two more pieces of the puzzle before he could start his new business. First, he needed four above-ground mechanical pumps that would lift the gasoline from the underground tanks, and without money to invest, he needed them at a low price. The source was a shade tree mechanic in Clinton, Oklahoma, named Bob Luffman, who specialized in restoring old gas pumps in his back yard. Once he had them in place, Luffman could keep them serviced.

Second, Tom needed people to run his start-up business. For a support staff, he turned to Judy, who was well organized and had a gift for numbers. Tom, who years later would confess he did not even balance his own check book, relied on Judy for many years to collect money, pay the bills, and prepare profit and loss statements. For the first three years, she worked from a metal roll-top desk in a bedroom of their 1,100- square-foot house in Oklahoma City.

For day-to-day management at the service station, Tom hired a thirty-eight year old local man named Stan Schroeder. The grandson of German immigrants, Stan was a big man who was raised on a farm five and a half miles east of Okarche. After the eighth grade, he quit school to farm the family's three quarter-sections, but left the farm in the 1950s to work as a lineman for Cimarron Electric Cooperative based in Kingfisher. In 1963, when he met Tom Love, Stan was working as a lineman out of the company's office in Watonga. Although the details of his management contract are lost in the haze of history, his compensation probably consisted of a small salary in the range of $100 a week plus a few pennies for every gallon of gasoline sold. The hours of operation would be 7:00 am to 11:00 pm seven days a week.

As the day approached for the opening of the service station, Tom contracted with a common carrier truck driver to pick up and deliver his first load of gasoline. When the driver arrived at the refinery gate, he was asked for proof that the new company had a bond to cover the motor fuel tax that would be owed to the State of Oklahoma on the twentieth of every month. Tom, who could not afford to pay the tax up-front at the refinery, admitted he did not know he needed a bond.

With a sense of urgency, Tom went to one established insurance agency in Oklahoma City to purchase the necessary bond. The agent asked for a profit and loss statement. Tom said he did not have one. The agent asked for a business plan with capital invested and earnings projected. Tom said he did not have one. The agent, with a bit of attitude, said he could not sell him a bond, but he would be happy to sell him a liability policy. Tom declined and left.

He went to a phone booth and called another agency big enough to handle the motor fuel tax bond. Answering the phone call was Jimmy McEldowny, a World War II bomber pilot who had

Tom ran an advertisement (facing page) in the Watonga newspaper in January of 1964 announcing the newest business in town. Within a year, the little service station was carrying a small line of merchandise as well as gasoline. A local dairy provided milk (above).

been educated at Harvard before joining Ancel Earp's insurance firm in Oklahoma City. Jimmy treated Tom with respect and took him to lunch. As they talked about the plans for the service station, Jimmy recognized and respected the confidence Tom had in himself and his abilities to grow his business to other locations. He sold him the motor fuel tax bond and thereafter earned subsequent policies as the business grew.

With a load of gasoline, a manager, and a building, Tom opened that first service station on January 6, 1964. Ten days later, in the January 16, 1964, edition of the *Watonga Republican* newspaper, Tom ran a half-page advertisement that read:

"Knox Industries Proudly Announce the Opening of Our NEW SERVICE STATION...Stan Schroeder, Manager...the Best for Less... All oil company credit cards accepted...Products by Kerr McGee Oil Industries...Fuels for the Future." Reflecting the small town nature of the business, the advertisement included the cordial invitation, "Come by and visit with us...Watch for our big 'Grand' opening."

After months of planning, their first service station was open, but for Tom and Judy, there was no time to reflect on that success. They were already looking over the next horizon for another abandoned station.

The urge to expand and grow the business, which would become the cornerstone of his business philosophy, was due in part to Tom's optimism and confidence in himself, but mostly, it was a necessary component of his business plan to operate service stations with one overriding goal—to offer the cheapest gasoline in town. He did not care about flashy buildings, big signs, or advertising. The only thing that mattered was to be one or two cents a gallon cheaper than his competitors.

As a result of that inflexible goal, the profit margin on each gallon of gasoline was thin, given that labor costs were similar at all stations and the motor fuel tax was about half of the retail price. Besides keeping capital expenditures low, which Tom had done by finding an abandoned station and used equipment, there were two ways to generate a profit. One was to find low cost gasoline at the refinery, which was possible but risky. The other was to increase the volume of sales. Some increases could be achieved at any given service station with long hours, better service, and a great location, but that had its limits. The only way to substantially increase the volume of sales was to open more service stations. Tom, who understood that cold hard fact, became the agent for growth through more locations, while Stan ran the first station and Judy kept the books.

Tom found his next opportunity in the little town of Sayre, located in far western Oklahoma near the Texas border. It was a county seat town of approximately 3,000 people, similar in size to Watonga, with an economy based on farming, ranching, and stripper oil well production which in turn supported merchants, teachers, lawyers, and other townspeople. Tom leased an abandoned station on old Route 66, bought used equipment from Bob Luffman, and hired as his manager a local man named Buck York, the nephew of the celebrated World War I hero, Alvin York, made famous by the Howard Hawk movie starring Gary Cooper.

Over the next year, Tom found additional abandoned service stations in Elk City, Minco, Kingfisher, Cordell, and Clinton, all located in western Oklahoma and all on state or U.S. highways. The Clinton and Elk City stations were on Route 66, where traffic counts were higher but where the competition was tougher. The bell cow of the first six stations was in Kingfisher, a prosperous town of 4,000 people located at the junction of U.S. Highways 270 and 81. In the 1960s, Kingfisher not only had a good agricultural economy based on wheat, but also light industry, active oil exploration and production, and the headquarters of Pioneer Telephone Cooperative.

During those early years of expansion, Tom established a management style that would remain consistent as the company

> When Tom got home that night, he found a note written by his father: "Merry Christmas Tom. Remember, you've got the rest of your life to change the world, but you've only got one shot at raising these kids. Love, Dad."

grew. While he left day-to-day operations to others, he was the road warrior scouting for new locations, finding owners, negotiating leases, securing the best prices for gasoline at the refinery gate, and contracting with common carriers to haul the product to his stations. He soon realized that was too much for one person, a fact illustrated by a memory from his first Christmas in the business.

With six service stations opened, Tom decided he would reward his station managers for working on the holiday. On Christmas morning, he loaded his pickup with frozen turkeys, drove from store to store, and gave a turkey to each employee. While he was gone, his father and mother visited Judy and the two babies. When Tom got home that night, he found a note written by his father: "Merry Christmas Tom. Remember, you've got the rest of your life to change the world, but you've only got one shot at raising these kids. Love, Dad." Tom would never forget that lesson and thereafter rarely missed holidays or the activities of his children.

By 1970, the Love family included (from left to right) Frank, Jenny, Laura and Greg.

Skiatook (east), OK

Skiatook (west), OK

Kansas

Collinsville (east), TX

Cleveland (east), TX

After considering a move to Clinton, an idea that Judy vetoed, Tom turned system-wide operations management over to J.B. Nabors, the first manager of station #6 in Cordell. Nabors, like Stan Schroeder, was a country boy born in rural Washita County. He was thirty-two years old, five-feet seven-inches tall, with an outgoing personality. After serving two years in the Army, J.B. married and farmed until the late 1950s when he got a job working at a Deep Rock service station in Cordell. When Tom leased the station, he hired J.B. with a small salary and commission on gasoline sold. Within a year he was promoted to general manager with responsibilities for day-to-day operations at all of Tom's service stations.

Judy handled details at the other end of the operations. From their home in Oklahoma City, she collected checks from the service station managers, paid bills, and kept ledgers tracking profit and loss. Most importantly, she documented and paid the motor fuel tax that was due to the Oklahoma Tax Commission on the twentieth of the month. If she was late with the payment, Tom could not buy fuel at the refinery, but if she was early, it took cash out of their carefully balanced expansion plans.

To gain a day or two of extra cash, Judy moved her primary checking account every month to a new bank somewhere near one of their most distant service stations. Whether it was true or not, she believed that the extra distance from the Tax Commission offices in Oklahoma City might delay delivery of the check, which only had to be postmarked by midnight on the twentieth. Years later, Tom met Herman Rice, the director of the Oklahoma Motor Fuel Tax Department, who admitted he knew what Judy was doing, which was perfectly legal. He said it became a game in the office to guess where the next check would come from, including some places they did not know were on the map. Judy would continue keeping the books for more than a decade, and even when the company purchased a computer for profit and loss statements, she insisted on keeping a parallel system with paper and ink for more than a year.

Although Tom and Judy had a few nervous moments when the Tax Commission checks were due, they rarely lost money in any one month in the 1960s. Profits, on the other hand, were modest due to the constant reinvestment in new service stations, but they were steady. Years later, Judy would remember a few months when profits topped $5,000 and there was never a year in the red. By 1967, cash flow was good enough to lease a second floor office in a building on Wilshire east of May Avenue, which became the first headquarters of Musket Corporation, and they had made enough money and felt good enough about further prospects that they built a new home on 69th Terrace in Oklahoma City's Edgewater Addition in 1969. Seven days after moving into the new house, their third child, Jennifer Anne Love, was born, followed three years later by the birth of their second son, Frank Criner Love.

There were a few setbacks during those initial years of growth. Two years after the grand opening of the Knox Station in Watonga, Tom decided to replace the old buried tanks with new and larger tanks equipped with submersible pumps. The installation crews got the first tank buried, but left the tank hole open over the weekend. When it rained, the tank settled and the submersible pumps discharged 8,000 gallons of gasoline into the surrounding soil. As if that was not bad enough, Tom reported the disaster to the Tax Commission and asked whether or not he still had to pay the tax. They said yes, the tax was levied not on the gasoline sold, but on the gasoline lifted. He lost his investment in the gas and had to double that loss by paying the tax.

Another disaster hit his service station in Weatherford in 1968. The attendant put the pump nozzle into the tank of a car and switched it to automatic while he cleaned the windshield and checked the oil. With the pump still running, the attendant went into the office to collect from another customer. The driver of the car followed him in, said he did not want his tank topped off, and paid his bill. Before the attendant could get outside, the man drove off with the pump nozzle in the tank and the pump exploded. The driver stopped, pulled the nozzle out of his tank, and drove off. The service station burned to the ground.

Despite such disasters, the little chain of service stations continued to grow, and as it grew, the logistics of using common carrier truck lines to get gasoline from the refinery to stations

Stroud, OK

From 1964 to 1972, Tom opened a string of service stations across Western Oklahoma and Southern Kansas (above and facing page). Although most were branded as Deep Rock or Knox, a few retained other signs. Tom would later refer to them as the "no name" stations.

One of Tom's first station managers, Bill Riech, expanded the Watonga location with extra pumps and bigger tanks as sales increased in the late 1960s.

became more complex and time consuming. One solution would have been to use local jobbers, but that would have cut into Tom's already thin profit margin and threatened his ability to provide the cheapest gasoline in town. Another option would have been to buy a truck and hire a person to serve as a combined dispatcher/truck driver who would be responsible for getting the right amount of gasoline to each station when they needed it. The last thing Tom wanted was a station that ran out of gasoline. Unfortunately, he did not yet have the scale of operations or the capital investment to make that work. He needed a trucking partner who would provide logistical efficiencies, but carry bills until the gasoline was sold. In 1966 Tom found that partner in Keith Price.

A decade older than Tom, Keith had grown up in Oklahoma City where his family operated Price and Sons Grocery. He served with General George Patton's 3rd Army during World War II, assisted the prosecution of war criminals after the war, and returned home where he got a job as a truck dispatcher with Save-More Oil Company. Years later, Keith remembered that coordinating the little fleet of 4,000-gallon, single- axle trucks loaded with gasoline, batteries, cans of oil, and other merchandise taught him the value of relationships with drivers, employees, and customers.

In the mid-1960s, Enid-based Champlin Oil Company bought Save-More Oil but sold the trucks to Western Commercial Transport, an interstate diversified tank company owned by Amon Carter. When Carter asked Keith to move to Fort Worth, he declined the offer and resigned. In 1966, with one truck owner/operator willing to join

Bill Rieck and his three children (facing page) posed for a photograph in front of the old Knox service station in Watonga that had been transformed into a small store and deli by enclosing the two service bays (left) and adding a rustic mansard roof.

him, Keith created a new trucking venture called Oklahoma Tank Lines. He quickly used his relationships to haul gasoline for Kerr-McGee, which in turn lead to an opportunity to meet Tom Love. For the next thirty years, Keith Price would deliver most of Tom's gasoline and become one of his best friends at the same time.

Tom's willingness to delegate responsibility to others, both in duties and creative freedom, was an important key to his emerging management style as the chain of full-service gasoline stations grew to more than forty communities in western Oklahoma. A good example of this trust was his relationship with an employee and subsequent competitor, Bill Rieck.

Typical of Tom's early employees, Bill was a hard working country boy. He was born in 1937 near Southard, Oklahoma, and attended a number of schools growing up before finishing high school in Watonga. His first job outside the home was working in the Mobil service station at the four corners intersection. He was twelve years old at the time. After a semester at the University of Oklahoma, he worked in a mine in Washington state, bought a new car, and returned to Oklahoma where he attended college for another year before getting married.

During the late 1960s, Tom transformed another of his stations in Laverne, Oklahoma, with a new roof, new pumps, and an increasing line of food and merchandise.

In 1957, Bill worked as an independent contractor gathering milk from farmers in the Watonga area. Using his own truck and bobtail trailer, he drove up and down country roads picking up milk in five and ten-gallon containers and delivering the loads to the Gold Spot Dairy in Enid. He made enough money to buy a new car and a boat. He also purchased two combines and worked the wheat harvest on surrounding farms. In 1965, when he heard that Stan Schroeder was quitting his job running Tom Love's Knox service station in Watonga, he applied for and got the job.

As a country entrepreneur accustomed to doing a little bit of everything to get ahead, Bill liked the independent nature of running the service station. Tom came by often, but left the day-to-day operations to his managers who earned a monthly salary plus a few cents for every gallon of gasoline sold. Bill also earned extra money for light mechanical work, washing cars, and selling merchandise such as windshield wipers, tires, and soda pop. Assisting him was his wife, Donna, who kept the books and worked the station when needed, and a part time employee named Allen Dixon, a hard working state highway department employee who covered the station evenings and on weekends. During wheat harvest in the spring and summer, Bill did triple duty farming 160 acres and keeping his combines cutting on surrounding farms.

Motivated by the possibility of sharing increased profits, Bill gradually added more merchandise to the service station. He started with milk and bread, which could be ordered from local vendors, and eventually took out a license to sell beer. Years later, he fondly remembered one hot Fourth of July weekend when he sold an entire truck load of beer in one day. Another profit generator added to the service station was a coin-operated ice machine leased from a vendor in Woodward. Then he approached Tom about a major expansion of merchandise.

If he could enclose the wash and lift bays for more floor space, Bill thought he could add a full line of take-out food, which would create additional income and attract customers needing gasoline. Tom agreed to pay for the improvements. Once the bays were enclosed with glass, Bill and his wife opened a full deli operation with fried chicken, ribs, and Polish sausage ordered from an Oklahoma City meat processing firm called Schwab. Some days Bill cleaned the chickens and his wife fried them. Other days she cleaned and he fried.

By 1970, the management arrangement between Tom and Bill reached a tipping point. Tom, who still saw gasoline sales as his primary profit center, did not yet want to expand further into

Tom's willingness to delegate responsibility to others, both in duties and creative freedom, was an important key to his emerging management style as the chain grew to more than forty communities in western Oklahoma.

food and groceries while he was still adding service stations to his system. Bill, who liked the possibilities of increased food service, thought he could do better with more space and total control of the business plan. As a result, Bill quit the Knox station, purchased a vacant Nash car dealership across the street, and opened a small grocery store called the Superette. As Bill would admit almost fifty years later, he "wanted to chase his own rabbits."

Over the next two years, Bill added profit centers to his own store. In addition to a full line of groceries, he installed full-service gasoline pumps under the Skelly brand, developed a take-out deli similar to

Tom (at far right) joined Oklahoma veterans such as Barney Brown to promote the gasoline distribution industry. When the Arab Oil Boycott sent shock waves through the market place, Tom stepped forward as an industry leader and offered testimony in Washington, D.C. (facing page).

what he had done across the street, and built a two-bay car wash. One was a self-service wand-wash that cost a quarter. The other was a drive-through "Triple Clean" automatic wash that cost seventy-five cents. He also added a self service ice machine with its own chipper and bagger.

In 1972, hungry for even greener pastures, Bill wanted to buy a nearby business called the Red Barn Cafe. His plan was to expand into food service and open a chain of restaurants. He approached Tom, told him of his plan, and offered to sell the grocery store. At the time, Tom was already considering expansion into the convenience store business, so he agreed to buy the grocery store across the street from his service station. Tom bought a new sign and renamed the grocery store Big Top Foods.

As Tom was concluding the deal to buy the Superette, he asked Bill to take a trip with him to Stillwater. Tom shared his plans for

building a new type of store, a combination service station and convenience store, similar to what Bill had done with the Superette, and he needed someone to run the operations side of the business while he focused on expansion and construction of new stores. He offered the job to Bill. When Bill asked if he would be a partner, Tom said no, Musket Corporation was a family-owned business. Years later, Bill would recall Tom's counter offer word for word. "You won't be a partner," Tom said, "but if you take the job I will make you richer than a banker." Bill thanked him for the confidence, but said no, he wanted to own his own business. They parted friends.

The Superette was a modest investment for Tom, done partly to control competition across the street from his Knox Service Station, but it provided two links to his future success. One was a recent college graduate who was the assistant manager at the Superette. The other was the sales representative for Affiliated Foods, the Tulsa-based wholesale distributor that stocked the Superette with food and merchandise.

After eight years of building a business based on the cheapest gas in town, Tom and Judy were ready for their next challenge.

The Love family grew alongside the business. This family portrait was taken in the 1970s with (clockwise) Tom, Laura, Greg, Judy, Frank, and Jenny.

THE COUNTRY STORE

By 1971, Tom and Judy Love had good reason to be pleased with the results of their hard work opening and operating a string of full-service gas stations across Oklahoma. They had found a niche in a highly competitive business dominated by major oil companies. They had overcome their lack of investment capital by focusing on low margin, high volume sales supported by cash flow. Most important, they had learned critical lessons.

Through experience, Tom recognized his own strengths and weaknesses.

He admitted he was an optimist, always seeing the bright side of any situation, which reinforced his willingness to work hard and bolstered his confidence that he could handle any situation, good or bad. He learned to trust his natural ability to build relationships with people, whether they were competitors, bankers, vendors, or employees, which in turn gave him a chance to listen to others and depend on a wide circle of friends.

At the same time, Tom realized he was not a detail oriented manager willing to run a business one day, one moment at a time. He was better, he knew, at looking over the next horizon as an agent of growth who was never satisfied with past achievements. On the back side of that trajectory, he needed people who could take the pieces of the puzzle he brought to the table and put them together in the most efficient, profitable way. He needed managers who could execute his vision and add their own energy and ideas.

After almost seven years in the business, Tom also realized that the retail sale of gasoline offered limited opportunities for growth. With fierce competition and a glut of cheap imported oil flowing into refineries, the already thin profit margin would never get any better. What he needed was a way to use the assets and experience he had already accumulated and add another profit center to gasoline sales. He needed a concept he could use in the small towns he knew so well and take advantage of his growing instinct for selecting good locations.

He called his solution to that challenge the Country Store.

The Country Store was a fusion of existing business models adapted to the specific needs of small towns in rural Oklahoma. In many ways, Tom wanted a small grocery store with a full line of merchandise from canned food and paper products to dairy items and baked goods. Going up against national chains like Safeway and locally owned independents such as IGA and United, he knew the Country Store could not compete in variety or cost, but it could compete in hours of operation. Tom would keep his little stores open from 7:00 am in the morning to 11:00 pm at night, seven days a week, at a time when many tradition-bound, small town merchants closed at 5:00 pm in the afternoon and did not open on Sundays.

The hours of operation, combined with the small quantities of goods and higher prices, would be more like a traditional convenience store. The most popular urban-based convenience store chain in the nation at the time had been founded in 1927 at a string of retail ice docks owned by the Southland Corporation in Dallas, Texas. By the 1930s, the ice docks were called Tote'm Stores, where customers "toted" away cold products such as eggs, milk, pop, and beer. In 1946, as the stores spread into suburban neighborhoods and expanded hours from early morning to late at night, the name was changed to 7-Eleven. By 1965, the little chain had grown to more than 3,500 stores coast-to-coast, located primarily in big and medium sized cities. Tom thought he could make the concept work in small towns.

Tom's concept also included gasoline sales with the twist of self-service. Although rare, self-service was not new. Like so much associated with car culture, self-service filling stations had started in Southern California. Out of 81,000 service stations located

around the country in 1951, approximately 200 were advertised as "self service." Some communities and a few states banned self-service, citing safety concerns, but generally the opposition reflected the political power of major oil companies developing their own full-service branded stations in the 1950s and 1960s. A critical new tool making self-service more convenient and common in the 1960s was a remote control unit inside stores that displayed the amount and cost of gas pumped and allowed a person at the cash register to reset and control the pumps.

For the location of his first combination grocery/convenience store/self-service gas station, Tom chose the town of Guymon, an economic, political, and transportation hub of approximately 6,000 people in the middle of the Oklahoma Panhandle. In addition to ranching and feedlots, the local economy was boosted by production from the surrounding Hugoton Oil Field, two carbon black plants, and a Phillips Petroleum gas plant. Most important to Tom, Guymon was located at the junction of three U. S. highways, 54, 64, and 412, and two state highways, 3 and 36. In the fall of 1971, at the north approach into town at 12th Street and Main, he found and leased an abandoned Texaco service station from George Vestal, a local businessman.

Tom tackled the remodeling of the station with the assistance of J. B. Nabors, his roving manager from Cordell who had helped keep the service stations running. They kept the gas pumps and underground storage tanks that were already in place, but enclosed the service bays, installed coolers, and added canopies over the gas pumps. They bought shelving, added a cash register and remote pump control unit, and upgraded the bathrooms that were accessed from the exterior of the building on the north side. Finally, they installed a sign with the name "Mini-Stop Country Store," which reflected the small size, quick service, and small town markets in rural areas Tom knew so well.

With a good location and a remodeled building, Tom needed a manager. The first prerequisite was someone with retail experience who was local. He wanted the Country Store to feel like a small town grocery, a place where the manager could build relationships with customers to add value to convenience and location. Some of the mom and pop groceries operating at the time were still owned by people who sat next to their customers at church and carried charge accounts paid at the end of the month. To compete with those local ties, Tom's manager needed to counter strength with similar strength. He found just what he needed in Fred and Janice Sledge.

Fred and Janice were natives of Guymon. Fred's parents had operated a Sinclair service station for thirty years, so he had experience in retail sales and gasoline distribution. Janice's mother operated a beauty parlor, so she was well connected socially. After graduating from high school in 1962, Fred attended Panhandle State College, but quit during his senior year to marry Janice. His first full-time job was a parts manager at the local Chevrolet dealership. When it sold to new management after five years, he worked in the oil patch for a year until he saw a newspaper advertisement seeking a manager for a new type of convenient grocery store. He applied, drove to Oklahoma City for an interview with Tom Love, and became the first manager of a Country Store. His salary was $150 a week, matched by another $150 a week for his wife, who worked the second shift from 3:00 pm to 11:00 pm.

The husband and wife management team helped Tom and J.B. Nabors find vendors to stock the little store. The gasoline would come from a terminal in Laverne, located about ninety-six miles to the east, and deliveries would be made by Oklahoma Tank Lines. Grocery items, including tobacco products, would come from Longbotham's Wholesale Company, founded in Guymon during the 1930s. Two route salesmen, operating from a 7,500-square-foot warehouse, not only took orders but also stocked the shelves.

Dairy products, which had a shorter shelf life and tended to turn over more rapidly, came from Deakin's Dairy located on the outskirts of Guymon. Bread, another item that had to be replaced daily, came from a local supplier as well. Beer, which would prove to be one of the most profitable products sold at the store, came from regional distributors. Years later, Fred would fondly remember the Coors truck that delivered his best selling brand of beer. The only product a customer could not find in the Mini-Stop Country Store

Tom acknowledged the importance of everyday repeat customers with an aggressive advertising campaign for the first several months after opening.

When the first Mini-Stop Country Store opened in Guymon in 1971 (previous spread), Tom ran a weekly advertisement in the local newspaper establishing a brand for a new kind of business with a mix of self-service gasoline and a variety of food and merchandise. In short, it was a "country store."

IT'S A REAL PLEASURE

TO TELL YOU ABOUT...

THE

MINI-STOP

COUNTRY

STORE

WE'RE OPEN 16 HOURS A DAY, EVERY DAY INCLUDING SUNDAYS AND HOLIDAYS, WE OPEN AT 7 A.M. AND CLOSE AT 11 P.M. WE'RE LOCATED AT THE CORNER OF 12th & N. MAIN AND...

COME IN AND SEE US!

ATTENTION LADIES

TRY IT! YOU'LL LIKE IT! AND YOU'LL SAVE MONEY

Drive In To The Mini-Stop At 12th & Main Next Time You Need Gasoline. If You Need Assistance At Our Self Service Pumps, We'll Be Glad To Help You.

See Our New Western Hats, Many Sizes And Colors For Pioneer Days. And... We Also Have A Large Variety Of Picnic Supplies. Come In And Look Around!

MINI-STOP COUNTRY STORE

OPEN 7 DAYS A WEEK — 7 A.M. TO 11 P.M.

MORE NEWS ABOUT...

THE

MINI-STOP

COUNTRY

STORE

OPEN 7 DAYS A WEEK 7 A.M. TO 11 P.M.

Good Selection Of **PANTY HOSE** Lots Of Sizes And Colors	Yes! We Have It! **REFRIGERATED** SHOAL & COPENHAGEN **SNUFF**

TRY OUR GASOLINE
Simply Turn Lever On Pump And Put In Amount You Want. Come Inside To Pay

FRED SLEDGE
MANAGER

IN THE **Good Old Days**

IN THE GOOD OLD DAYS THERE WERE COUNTRY STORES. NOW, THERE'S THE

MINI-STOP

COUNTRY STORE

"Good Selection Of Anything You Need"!

★ LOTS OF COLD BEER - ALL BRANDS

★ Plenty Of Ice   ★ Icees   ★ Cold Pop   ★ Discount Gasoline
★ All Kinds of Foods & Supplies For Your Week-End Picnic

OPEN 7 DAYS A WEEK — 7 A.M. TO 11 P.M. -Corner of 12th & Main

MORE NEWS ABOUT...

THE

MINI-STOP

COUNTRY

STORE

OPEN 7 DAYS A WEEK 7 A.M. TO 11 P.M.

ICE 5-lb. BAG **25¢**	**COLD BEER**

DISCOUNT GAS
Come In And Let Us Show You How Easy It Is To Serve Yourself At The Gas Pump

FRED SLEDGE
MANAGER

ATTENTION LADIES

TRY IT! YOU'LL LIKE IT! AND YOU'LL SAVE MONEY

Drive In To The Mini-Stop At 12th & Main Next Time You Need Gasoline. If You Need Assistance At Our Self Service Pumps, We'll Be Glad To Help You.

We Now Have "ICEE"
While You're Here, See Our New Case Of Novelty Items Including Italian Sunglasses, Etc.

The Coldest Drink In Town!

MINI-STOP COUNTRY STORE

OPEN 7 DAYS A WEEK — 7 A.M. TO 11 P.M.

Tom, of course,
was thrilled with the
success of the first
Country Store.
Instead of satisfaction,
however, all he
thought of were
the possibilities.

was fresh produce, which had a high profit margin but was risky with a high rate of spoilage.

On January 20, 1972, a front-page story in the *Guymon Daily Herald* served notice that a new store had opened in town. "The Mini-Stop Country Store is now open at the corner of 12th and Main," said Fred Sledge, manager. "Featured are national advertised brands of groceries and household items," he added, "and gas pumps are presently being installed and will be ready at a later date." The reporter noted that the store had one unusual feature. The hours of operation would be 7:00 am to 11:00 pm, seven days a week, including holidays. In little towns like Guymon, where blue laws restricting hours and days of retail sales were still on the books but seldom enforced, that announcement must have raised a few eyebrows.

Although Tom was counting on a customer base that included a combination of local residents and the traveling public, he acknowledged the importance of everyday repeat customers with an aggressive advertising campaign for the first several months after opening. On February 9, 1972, his first advertisement ran in the newspaper, a two-column ad that served as a introduction to local people: "It's a real pleasure to tell you about the Mini-Stop Country Store." The simple copy then defined the qualities that gave the store an advantage against the competition: "We're open 16 hours a day, every day including Sundays and holidays. We open at 7 A.M. and close at 11 P.M....We're located at the corner of 12th and N. Main...come in and see us!"

Over the next several months, the advertisements ran at least once a week and defined the Country Store beyond the unique schedule. Each ad expanded on the products and services a person could find at the Country Store. First came "5-lb. Bag of Ice 25 cents" and "Cold Beer." That was followed the next week with "Good selection of pantyhose...lots of sizes and colors." Another feature boasted, "Yes We have it!...Refrigerated Skoal and Copenhagen Snuff." At the bottom of most ads ran a reminder that people could shop and fill their car with gasoline at the same place: "Try our gasoline...simply turn lever on pump and put in amount you want. Come in to Pay." Another offered "Discount gas...come in and let us show you how easy it is to serve yourself at the gas pump." Providing a personal touch in most ads was a salutation from "Fred Sledge, Manager."

Two months after the grand opening, an ad for the Country Store specifically targeted women in Guymon: "Attention Ladies... Try it…You'll like it…And you'll save money…Drive into the Mini-

Oklahoma Oil marketer

NOVEMBER-DECEMBER, 1970

By 1970, even before the first Country Store opened, Tom was recognized as an industry leader in fuel distribution and sales. Here, he was featured on the cover of the trade association's magazine.

Stop at 12th and Main next time you need gasoline. If you need assistance at our self service pumps, we'll be glad to help you." The image of the Country Store as a one-stop shopping experience was emphasized in the same ad with a boxed notice: "See our new western hats. Many sizes and colors for Pioneer Days. And...We also have a large variety of picnic supplies. Come in and look around." As always, the ad featured the strongest marketing tool: "Open 7 Days a Week...7 A.M. to 11 P.M."

Advertising for the Country Store alternated basic branding with new products. One week, half the ad featured a little bear drinking from a straw with the announcement, "We now have 'Icee'...the Coldest Drink in Town." The text added "While you're here, see our new case of novelty items including Italian sunglasses, etc." Another ad started with the banner headline, "In the Good Old Days There were Country Stores...Now, there's the Mini-Stop

Country Store...Good selection of anything you need...Plenty of ice, Icees, cold pop, discount gasoline."

Within three months, Tom knew the Mini-Stop Country Store far exceeded the profitability of his little service stations. Not only did he have a new profit center in groceries, but he also had a winner in self-service gasoline, still sold "at the cheapest price in town." Fred started calling Tom every other day with the same plea, "I am almost out of gasoline again." The tanks that came with the leased service station held only 5,000 gallons, but Fred was selling up to 3,000 gallons a day. Tom and J.B. Nabors came to the rescue and installed 10,000-gallon tanks. Years later, Fred would remember one month in 1974 when he sold 88,000 gallons of gasoline.

Tom, of course, was thrilled with the success of the first Country Store. Instead of satisfaction, however, all he thought of were the possibilities. Now he wanted more.

While the Sledges were experimenting with advertising, product selection, and operations, Tom once again was the road warrior looking over the next hill. The success of the first Country Store in Guymon convinced him he was going the right direction with the small grocery store with convenient hours and self-service gasoline, so he started looking for additional locations where the concept would work. He found one to the west and one to the east of Guymon, within reasonable driving distance for the wholesale distributors.

The second Country Store opened in Boise City, Oklahoma, the county seat of Cimarron County located at the geographical epicenter of the Dust Bowl that had devastated the region in the 1930s. It was 340 miles northwest of Oklahoma City, but was closer to two other state capitals in Santa Fe, New Mexico and Denver, Colorado. By 1972, Boise City had a population of approximately 1,800 people, but most importantly, it was located at the junction of five U.S. highways, 287, 385, 412, 64, and 56, and two state highways, 3 and 325. Tom leased an old service station on the approach into town from the east and remodeled it similarly to what he had done in Guymon.

The third Country Store opened in another remodeled service station in Buffalo, Oklahoma, the county seat of Harper County located due east of Guymon. It was at the junction of U.S. Highway 183, the route north from Woodward, Oklahoma to Dodge City, Kansas, and U.S. Highway 64, which ran east and west from the Panhandle to Enid and Tulsa. The little town of approximately 1,500 people was a regional market center that depended on farming, ranching, and some oil play. The Mini-Stop Country Store in Buffalo opened during the summer of 1972, followed quickly by another Country Store in Lamar, Colorado, the first outside the boundaries of Oklahoma.

Initial results from the Country Stores exceeded Tom's expectations. The amount of gasoline sold doubled what he was selling at his low-cost service stations, while the food items added another profit center without adding to labor costs. After years of struggling to make a trickle of money from marginal service stations, suddenly he saw real opportunity in front of him. There was only one problem. He needed managerial help, both on the operations side with merchandise and personnel and on the development end with general contractors. If he was going to expand with more Country Stores, especially those that would have to be built from the ground up, he needed reinforcements for day-to-day operations so he would have the freedom to find new locations and seek financing for new construction.

This gap in his organization led to Tom's conversation with Bill Rieck in September of 1972. Bill, who had once worked for Tom managing the service station in Watonga, had shown his operational skills by opening the take-out deli and building the competing Superette across the street. When Tom offered him a job as operations manager over the service stations and the new Country Stores, Bill said no, he had just bought the Red Barn Cafe in Watonga and wanted to own and manage his own business. Tom kept looking.

About the same time, an account manager for the wholesale house providing merchandise for the little Superette in Watonga came to town to do a complete inventory so they could tally a final bill for Bill Rieck and set up a new account with Tom Love. Over the course of several conversations, Tom and the account manager got to know each other. Tom shared his plan not only for the Superette, which he soon would rename Big Top Grocery, but also for the little chain of Mini-Stop Country Stores he wanted to expand. The fellow asked Tom if he had an operations guy. Tom said no, "we are just feeling our way into it and trying to learn the business." Tom, in return, asked the fellow, "Would you be interested in taking such a position?" The fellow asked for time to think about it and left.

That night, after reflecting on the conversations and his impression of the man, Tom called him at his home in Tulsa and formally offered him a job. Tom told him he thought the job was worth $800 a month. The account manager countered with $1,000. They talked some more and Tom agreed the job might be worth $1,000 a month. By the end of the telephone call he had a new operations manager. The man's name was Larry Dillard.

Larry Dillard (left) had worked in both grocery stores and a wholesale grocery supply business when he met Tom Love. His skill sets in marketing, operations, and inventory control complemented Tom's entrepreneurial skills and knowledge of the gasoline distribution business.

Larry Dillard started working in a Safeway Grocery as a teenager. By the age of nineteen, he was already a store manager. One of Larry's hobbies was ham radio (below).

Larry, nine years older than Tom, was raised during the hard times of the Great Depression. He spent his early years on the family farm four miles south of Pauls Valley, but moved back and forth several times from Oklahoma to Arizona with his family during the 1930s. His jobs as a kid included milking cows, helping a man sell newspaper subscriptions to farm families for twenty-five cents a day and a meal, and working at Vaught's Grocery and Market in Pauls Valley. His first task every morning was to kill, pluck, and dress chickens.

At the age of fifteen, while in Arizona, Larry got a job working at Safeway for fifteen cents an hour after school and a ten-hour shift on Saturdays. During the war, he always had a job but made more money buying and selling used cars at a time when new cars were not being made. As the war came to an end, he took a full time job with the Safeway in Pauls Valley, Oklahoma, working a seventy-two-hour week for $18, which went up to $35 a week after the war. At the age of nineteen, he was named store manager.

Larry remained with Safeway for thirteen years, working his way up through larger stores in the region and gaining management experience working within a system that balanced profit margins and labor costs with efficient operations and customer service. In 1959, he left Safeway to join Scrivners, a large regional wholesale grocery firm, which led to a job with Affiliated Foods headquartered in Tulsa. He was an account manager when he met Tom Love at the little Superette grocery store in Watonga.

Larry's first task as operations manager for Musket Corporation was to standardize the way the Country Stores and the one grocery store in Watonga were being managed. He wrote an operations manual with policies, procedures, and clearly defined duties. He

got to know the managers and their second shift workers. He adjusted displays and set new prices. Most importantly, he freed Tom's schedule by taking over hiring and disciplinary responsibilities, getting a handle on accountability in a cash-based business, and planning for the opening of new locations.

One of Larry's first major changes in the business plan was to use Affiliated Foods in Tulsa, Oklahoma, as a wholesale provider for groceries and general merchandise. Affiliated had been organized in 1939 as a cooperative wholesale house owned jointly by ten independent grocery store owners in the Tulsa area who were fighting back against aggressive national chains such as Safeway. By the 1960s, with independent grocers losing that battle, Affiliated Foods developed a specialty in serving convenience stores across the region. For the Mini-Stop Country Stores, Affiliated Foods provided not only a convenient one-stop source for wholesale goods and weekly delivery, but also a quiet partner who helped with displays, product selection, and marketing tips.

With only a few stores, it did not take long for Larry to get a handle on daily routines. Typically, the store manager arrived at work at 6:00 am, checked gas levels in the tanks, completed paperwork such as reports and ordering, and opened the store at 7:00 am. The manager worked alone until 2:00 pm, when the hourly shift person arrived for duty and gave him or her a chance to get to the bank, restock shelves, and clean the facility. The manager then went home about 4:00 pm and returned at 10:00 pm to run the store for the last hour and close. The routine started again the next morning.

Larry quickly put his personal stamp on the operational philosophy of the Country Stores. Like Tom, he had a gift for motivating

"Larry did not worry about numbers," one long time associate recalled years later. "He said take care of the people and the numbers will take care of themselves."

Re-branded as a Love's Country Store, this location typified the early layout that allowed one staff person to manage the entire operation. The check out counter was to the right of the front door, which provided security and offered a view of the gas pumps through the side window.

people, but whereas Tom did that with his energetic optimism and good cheer, Larry did it with clear expectations and a hard-nosed demand for consistency. "Larry did not worry about numbers," one long time associate recalled years later. "He said take care of the people and the numbers will take care of themselves." By that, he meant if managers would take care of their customers and their employees, everything else would fall into place. "Larry was a forceful, confident guy," Tom Love recalls. "He was six-feet-two inches tall, weighed about 230 pounds, and he could read people." According

The Arab Oil Embargo may have been a short term problem for gasoline distributors, but for entrepreneurs such as Tom Love, the crisis offered opportunities to take a risk while competitors waited for better times.

to Tom, if Larry instinctively mistrusted someone, he did not want them in his organization. Larry instantly trusted one of the employees he inherited. That young man was Harold Wells.

Harold was the son of an oil field driller, which in Oklahoma meant the family was nomadic. As a youth, Harold lived in Texas, Arkansas, central Oklahoma, northwestern Oklahoma, and southeastern Oklahoma, before graduating from high school in Watonga. In the fall of 1969, he commuted to Southwestern State College in Weatherford and worked part time for area farmers. In January of 1972, Bill Rieck hired him to work a full forty-hour work week at the Superette across the street from Tom Love's Knox service station.

During the week, Harold typically left for Weatherford and his classes on campus at 7:00 am in the morning and returned to Watonga by 3:00 pm to work an eight-hour shift until 11:00 pm that night. On Sundays he started at 7:00 am and worked through the noon hour rush at the deli. By September of 1972, when Bill sold the grocery store to Tom, Harold was the assistant manager who had been running the store when Bill was on vacation.

Larry Dillard recognized Harold's work ethic and appreciated the discipline needed to earn his college degree in math and physics while working full time at the store. In May of 1973, when a new Mini-Stop Country Store was being built in Springfield, Colorado, Larry asked Harold if he would in effect be his district manager and handle the stocking, opening, and training at the new store. Accustomed to a nomadic life, he took the assignment. For almost two months, Harold lived in a motel and spent every day at the new store. He helped Larry interview prospective managers and trained the man selected, Paul Looker, who had been delivering milk for a regional dairy. Looker's wife was hired as the second shift assistant manager. In Harold Wells, Larry and Tom had a man they could depend on in the field.

Another thing Tom could depend on was unexpected change. In the fall of 1973, just as he was putting together his plan and team for the Country Stores, one of the most dramatic turning points in the economic history of the United States threatened that future. It was the Arab Oil Embargo of 1973.

The stage for the energy crisis had been coming together for several decades. In 1960, in an effort to gain a competitive advantage when dealing with the large multi- national oil companies from the United States, Great Britain, and the Netherlands, twelve countries in the developing world banded together to form OPEC, the Organization of the Petroleum Exporting Countries. The informal bargaining coalition included seven Arab countries plus Venezuela, Indonesia, Nigeria, and Ecuador.

The ticking time bomb was primed by rising oil consumption in the developed world, especially the United States where the use of oil was increasing almost five percent a year in the 1960s. With cheap imported oil reducing the incentive to explore and drill in the United States, domestic production peaked in 1970 and started a downward spiral. Adding to the volatile mixture of economics and politics was the world-wide abandonment of the gold exchange standard in 1971 and the global Cold War between the United States and the

In the fall of 1973, just as he was putting together his plan and team for the Country Stores, one of the most dramatic turning points in the economic history of the United States threatened that future.

NATIONAL PETROLEUM NEWS

FEBRUARY 1973

If the Worst Happens, Do You Have a Plan? Tom Love Doped Out All Things That Could Go Wrong. Sure Enough, They Did. But Tom Had a Plan... Page 38

This national magazine did a profile on Tom Love's ability to cope with challenges. Although he may not have expressed his philosophy this way in 1973, his strategy was based on one formula— growth creates opportunity.

Soviet Union. By the time Tom Love decided to expand beyond his little service stations and launch the Country Stores, the world was approaching a confluence of hyper-inflation, political brinkmanship, and a game-changing fight over the free flow of oil.

The "shot heard 'round the world" that set off this powder keg was the beginning of the Yom Kippur War on October 6, 1973. After Egypt and Syria invaded Israel, the Soviet Union sent arms and aid to the Arab countries while the United States rushed to protect Israel with weapons and supplies. Within two weeks, Libya, Saudi Arabia, and other oil-producing countries declared an embargo on oil shipments to the United States, which they considered an armed combatant. The result was panic, chaos, and a demand for immediate political action.

As the price of oil soared from three dollars to twelve dollars a barrel in the span of a few months, the perceived shortage was quickly translated into market and public overreaction. President Richard Nixon initially asked oil companies and service station operators to cease selling gasoline on Saturday evenings and on Sundays, which led to long lines at stations on weekdays. Rationing was attempted, with odd and even days based on license tag numbers. Coupons similar to World War II ration stamps were printed but never used. The national speed limit was reduced to fifty-five and daylight savings time was extended to the entire year. The crisis even convinced NASCAR to cancel the 24 Hours of Daytona.

President Nixon, trying to calm the panic and show that something was being done, appointed William E. Simon as the first Administrator of the Federal Energy Office. Although his agency would not be made a cabinet-level department until 1978, Simon was given broad powers to insert government control into the distribution of oil and gasoline during those early months of panic. A new battlefield was thus created, not with guns and bombs in the Middle East, but with lawyers and testimony in Washington, D.C. Tom Love, while trying to hold together his embryonic business and keep gasoline flowing to his customers, was thrust into the front lines of that battle.

Tom's role in the national dialog about energy was a matter of timing and willingness to serve. In 1964, when he opened his first service station, he joined the Oklahoma Oil Marketers' Association, a trade group that represented gasoline distributors across the state. Within five years, he rose to leadership positions as treasurer and president of the state group and director of the National Oil Jobbers Council (NOJC). In 1971, he was elected senior vice president of the national trade group with expectations that he would become president in 1975.

On December 16, 1973, accompanied by a photograph of a grim-looking Tom Love, a headline in *The Oklahoman* announced "City Oil Jobber to Advise FEA Officials." The FEA official was William Simon. Tom joined ten other jobbers from around the country who were asked to advise the Nixon Administration on "policy, legislation, and regulations to deal with the energy crisis." The big issues were price controls and restrictive allocations.

On the first front, Tom opposed short sighted policy that artificially protected consumers for a few months but damaged markets in the long run. On the second issue, Tom found himself and his fellow jobbers opposing major oil companies that wanted guaranteed distribution of gasoline to their own branded stations through allocation controls. "Government control of allocation was an impediment to a company like ours that was free-wheeling and really entrepreneurial," Tom recalled years later. "We were interested in growing as fast as we could and the majors were willing to hold onto what they had."

Tom was deeply involved in the national debate for three years, especially his first year as president of the NOJC. "We had a couple of really smart lawyers, Doug Mitchell and Bob Bassman, who attended hearings and followed legislation on the Hill," Tom remembered. "I testified numerous times before the energy committees of Henry "Scoop" Jackson in the U.S. Senate and John Dingle in the U.S. House of Representatives." While staff members focused on federal policies, Tom spent much of 1975 on the road communicating with the forty state associations at trade shows and annual conventions. He reported to members what was happening at the federal level, while he listened to them about their needs on the front lines of the marketplace.

Somehow, Tom managed to juggle his industry responsibilities with his leadership and operational roles at his own company. His most pressing task, like other jobbers, was to secure a steady supply of gasoline. The Federal Energy Administration initially froze allocations to stations at the levels sold the previous year, which hit Tom hard. Not only did each new Country Store more than double the amount of gasoline sold at any one of the old service stations, the allocations were based on the amounts of gasoline sold through contracts. To keep prices low, Tom had depended on distressed gasoline sold at the back gate without contracts.

When Tom told William Simon that he had been buying gasoline without contracts, Simon simply said, "you should have," but then pushed through an emergency provision to base allocations on what was lifted, not just sold on contract. An added burden to low-cost businesses like Love's Country Stores was the complex application for increased allocations that required an applicant to show a "public need," with maps indicating the location of competitors. One of the questions was, "Will your new station adversely affect the economic performance of competing stations?" To guarantee enough gas for even one new Country Store, Tom generally had to abandon two of his service stations and transfer the allocations.

Despite the end of the embargo in the spring of 1974, the energy crisis would continue for the rest of the 1970s as markets adjusted to the new realities of OPEC and energy companies ramped up efforts to find and produce more oil. To help him find a growing supply of gasoline at the lowest possible price during that turbulent time, Tom added another key person to his organization, a young man who was pursuing a Masters in Business Administration. His name was Terry Ross.

To guarantee enough gas for even one new Country Store, Tom generally had to abandon two of his service stations and transfer the allocations.

Born in Oklahoma City, Terry was the son of a geologist who specialized in the secondary recovery of oil through water flooding. They moved several times, going from one oil patch to another, but ended up in Texas where Terry attended the University of Texas and completed a degree in accounting. He moved back to Oklahoma City, enrolled in an MBA program, and supported himself painting houses in Nichols Hills. In April of 1976, when he saw an advertisement for an accounting job at Musket Oil Corporation, he applied for what he thought was a job with an oil exploration and production company. At the interview, Larry Dillard offered to give him a flexible schedule so he could finish his degree, so Terry took the job anyway.

The accounting department was still largely hand work in 1976, so Terry was assigned to the general ledger tabulating weekly reports from stores. He also helped with converting payroll to a small IBM computer. While handling those duties, he observed the way that Tom's secretary was handling the logistics of fuel supply. She would take reports from store managers, buy gasoline from familiar vendors, and schedule deliveries through Oklahoma Tank Lines. One thing Terry noticed was the high number of split loads, with part of a shipment delivered to one store and the rest delivered to another. He thought that was inefficient and said so. Tom said show him how he would improve the process. Within a few weeks, Tom had a new manager of fuel purchasing.

Terry created a system to help him anticipate demand. It started with trends based on inventory reports from managers who checked fuel levels every morning. As the data base grew, he would get reports, compare numbers to where they should be, and calculate the timing of when they would need a new load before running out. For purchasing, he developed a matrix of refineries, terminals, and jobbers where he could buy gasoline. He would find the best price, at a location nearest the store needing fuel, and dispatch an order to Oklahoma Tank Lines to deliver a full load when possible.

At the same time, Terry had to deal with allocation limits set by the Federal Energy Administration. "We never had enough allocation to keep up with demand," he remembered forty years later. Then there was the added pressure of Tom opening new Country Stores as Terry was trying to supply what they already had. When a new store opened in Miami, Oklahoma, it had an allocation of 4,000 gallons a month, which would not last even a week. Terry responded by finding gasoline supplies not just in the usual places, such as refineries and wholesale distributors, but also from unlikely sources like jobbers and independent service station operators

By the time the Arab Oil Embargo struck the nation, Love's Country Stores had a formula for success: low operational costs, clean bathrooms, and the cheapest gas in town. The challenge was keeping the tanks "wet" as many distributors closed when they ran out of gas.

willing to sell their allocations at a premium price and simply close their doors. Although the Country Stores had to sell the gasoline at a higher price to maintain profit margins, they had supplies when competitors did not. Fred Sledge, the manager at the first Country Store in Guymon, remembers that when other stations in town were out of gasoline, he always had a steady supply with a growing share of the market.

Inadvertently, this scrambling effort to maintain supplies created a problem that turned into an asset. When the Federal Energy Administration imposed allocation control, it included a

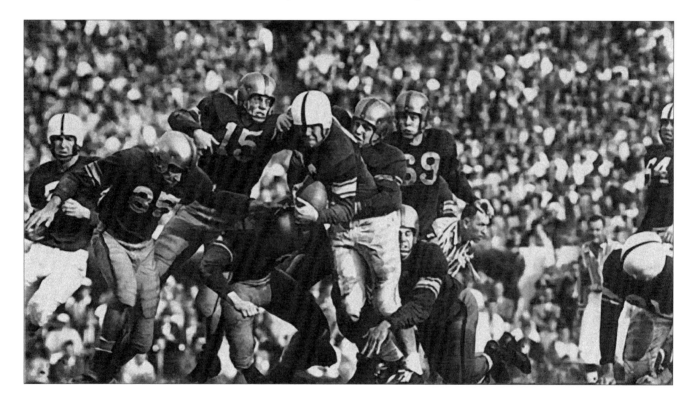

Lindell Pearson (carrying the football) was a celebrated running back for Bud Wilkinson's OU Sooners who went on to play in the NFL. Armed with a genial personality and good work ethic, he was the perfect colleague to implement Tom's aggressive strategy of expansion.

cap on profit margins frozen at the levels of the previous year. Terry and Tom interpreted that rule as the average profit margin of the combined service stations and Country Stores, not each individual point of sale. When FEA auditors ruled otherwise, arguing that the cap was to be calculated at each retail point of sale and not the system, Tom, without admitting fault, agreed to return the excess profits to his customers through lower prices and reduced margins. For several months, that gave Country Stores an even greater price advantage in their communities and helped increase the volume of sales and discourage potential competitors.

Just as the energy crisis was straining Tom's ability to find sources of gasoline for their service stations and Country Stores, he lost his field manager, J. B. Nabors, who had been with him since he opened the service station in Cordell. Larry Dillard had assumed some of the responsibilities for operations, especially in the convenience stores, but Nabors' departure created an organizational need for someone to help Tom in development of new locations. The person who filled that need was Lindell Pearson.

Lindell, only one generation removed from the farm, was a well known sports celebrity in Oklahoma. As a star athlete at Capitol Hill High School after World War II, he was aggressively recruited and signed by the University of Arkansas to play football, which motivated Virgil Browne, the owner of the Oklahoma City Coca-Cola bottling plant, to organize the University of Oklahoma Touchdown Club with the private resources to bring the star running back to Norman.

Two Oklahoma Highway Patrolmen drove to Fayetteville, Arkansas, where Lindell had already enrolled, and placed him in protective custody while Browne and his club co-founders delivered $4,000 to the Arkansas supporters who had invested in a home for the recruit's parents. For the next two years Lindell played for Coach Bud Wilkinson in the same backfield at the University of Oklahoma with quarterback Darrel Royal, fullback Leon Heath, and fellow halfback Junior Thomas. Although he lost one year of eligibility due to the transfer, he played another four years as running back for the Detroit Lions in the National Football League.

After a short stint as a football coach at Guthrie High School, Lindell took a job with Apco, an Oklahoma City-based energy company with operations scattered north and south along the Great Plains from Texas to South Dakota. He started as a sales representative working with independent jobbers selling Apco products and worked his way up the corporate ladder to district manager first in Kansas City and then in Nebraska. Just before the Arab Oil Embargo, he quit Apco to help a friend start a string of self-serve gas stations and convenience stores in St. Joseph, Missouri. When the energy crisis grounded that grand plan, he returned to Oklahoma City and a meeting with Tom Love, who jumped at the chance to hire the good natured and well known former football star.

By the end of 1974, although still in the shadows of the energy crisis, Tom was in a good position to redouble efforts at expansion. On the operational side, he had Larry Dillard running a tight ship with a growing support staff. On the supply side he had Affiliated Foods for groceries, Oklahoma Tank Lines for gasoline delivery, and Terry Ross scouring the countryside looking for enough fuel to preserve their reputation of having the cheapest gas in town. At the tip of the spear, he had Lindell Pearson helping him with site selection, financing, and supervision of contractors.

Tom also was well positioned on the playing field of the mar-

Lindell Pearson quickly adapted to his role as Tom's field general of growth.

ketplace. With rising fuel prices and limited allocations of gasoline, most competitors were merely trying to hang onto what they had rather than expanding with the great uncertainties still hanging low on the horizon. Tom, ever the optimist, ignored the clouds of doubt and saw only a clear field ahead.

Now all he needed were more sites, money to borrow, and new store managers.

As Tom was expanding his string of Country Stores, he carved out time to take family vacations that normally turned into road trips. The four kids would all remember stopping at stores along the way.

One expression of this renewed confidence in the future was a decision by Tom and Judy to build a new house. Their attorney, Tony Maguire, knew a physician who owned a two-and-three-quarter-acre lot in Nichols Hills he wanted to sell. They purchased it, had plans drawn up, and within eleven months had a 6,000-square foot home built by Everett Dale. The Love family moved into the home on July 8, 1975.

That fall, Judy quit working actively at the office and returned to college to finish her degree. This time, instead of journalism, she majored in interior design and completed her degree at Central State University in 1981. Two years later she earned her masters degree and started her own design firm. Although she was out of day-to- day operations, she remained secretary of the corporation and was in charge of all decorating for the company.

About the time Judy was thinking of returning to college, she and Tom decided to rebrand the convenience stores. In the fall of 1974, despite the need for a huge infusion of capital to fund their aggressive expansion plans, they wanted to reconfirm their commitment to keeping Musket Corporation a family-owned business and use the family name for their stores. Over the objection of Larry Dillard, who was a systems-oriented person who craved consistency, the name was changed from Mini-Stop Country Stores to Love's Country Stores.

New signs gradually were added to each of the locations. The main part of the sign, which was nine-feet wide and four-feet tall, was mounted on a twenty-foot-tall single pole clad in rough cedar. The name "Love's" was in script with "Country Store" below in block print. Below the primary sign on the left was another five-foot by four-foot sign where the price of gas was displayed in twenty-four-inch letters. On the right were three smaller four-foot signs stacked with the words, "Food," "Beer," and "Ice." Capping the entire array was a two-foot-tall flat roof faced with cedar shake shingles.

The new name, coupled with the adrenaline of surviving the

opening shock of the energy crisis, convinced Tom that he was on the right track with his aggressive expansion plans. Larry Dillard, who complemented Tom's vision for the future with his own focus on immediate, tangible details, had to slowly digest the concept of perpetual growth. Tom remembers one moment when he and his operations manager came to a pivot point of shared vision.

They were on the road when Tom mentioned to Larry that he had just purchased lots in another town for the fifteenth Love's Country Store. Larry, who could not see the logic in the timing or location selected by Tom, asked a direct question: "What do you have in mind in terms of growth, because I need to know where you think you're going...I thought that I was going to be able to run this operation with one district manager and myself, plus the store personnel." When Tom said, "Of course I am going to expand and I just assumed you knew that," Larry responded in his logical way. "I am going to have to shift gears mentally," he said, "and begin thinking about a larger organization and what it should look like." Forty years later, Tom remembered the critical importance of that conversation.

Lindell Pearson, on the other hand, quickly adapted to his role as Tom's field general of growth. After logging thousands of miles on the road with Tom, he installed an early version of a portable telephone in his car so he could stay in touch with all the players involved in multiple projects unfolding at the same time in different towns. His son remembers Lindell commonly leaving home at 3:30 am before sunup, hitting several small towns during the day, and returning late at night. Lindell's competitive temperament not only pushed him to keep up with Tom, but also saved money for the expanding company at times. Looking at lots in one small town, Tom told him to buy them at the listed price. Lindell thought he could do better, so he negotiated and saved several thousand dollars.

Tom remembers that Lindell treated others fairly, and in return, people liked him. That temperament served him well on construction sites, where the timing and sequencing of subcontractors was critical to keeping a project on schedule. Lindell had a way of convincing crews to work longer when necessary and adjust to the needs of the job. In one town, Lindell used his persuasive powers with a bank officer to ask for a loan to build another Country Store. When he was escorted into the bank president's office, he described the project and handed him Musket Corporation's profit and loss statement. When the bank president asked if it had been audited, Lindell simply said yes. The president looked at the loan officer and said, "Give him anything he wants."

About the time Judy was thinking of returning to college, she and Tom decided to rebrand the convenience stores. The name was changed from Mini-Stop Country Stores to Love's Country Stores.

"Son, I believe a banker has to look at the 3 C's—collateral, character, and cash flow—and while Tom Love does not have any collateral, I know his character and his cash flow is through the roof."

(Clinton banker F.A."Luke" Sewell's response when asked why he loaned Tom Love money without collateral.)

Although it was not part of some grand plan, Larry's and Lindell's learning curves were peaking at the perfect time, just as Tom was contemplating doubling the size of the Country Store chain in one bold move. The opportunity was created by a hostile takeover of the Oklahoma City-based energy firm, Apco, an integrated regional oil company founded by Lev Prichard and J. Steve Anderson in 1919. Highlights in the history of the locally venerated company included a gradual accumulation of oil production in four states, the purchase of the Cyril Refinery in southern Oklahoma in 1920, the purchase of the thirty-story-tall Ramsey Tower and renaming it as the Apco Tower in 1943, and expansion to more than 1,300 branded service stations. In 1977, after Northwest Energy Company gained a controlling block of stock, Apco was liquidated and the assets were either integrated into the new company or sold.

Tom purchased thirty-eight of the Apco stations located in small towns scattered across Oklahoma and Kansas. The average price paid for each property, including the land and improvements, was $35,000. His plan was to tear down the buildings and replace them with new, ground-up Love's Country Stores, each of which would cost approximately $150,000. Not only was this going to pose a challenge to the operational and logistical skills of Larry and Lindell, but it also would require a huge capital investment in the range of $6 million. Tom needed a new banker with the capital assets to take on the ambitious project.

Once again, the timing was right. By the mid-1970s, after years of hard work and constant expansion, Tom had both a profit and loss statement and enough net worth to borrow significant amounts of money for such improvements. As Tom would remember almost forty years later, he was never afraid of debt. The only question was who would loan it to him.

Some of his first small business loans had come from the First National Bank of Clinton, Oklahoma. Frank A. "Luke" Sewell, who purchased the country bank in 1935, had financed Tom's purchase of used gas pumps from Bob Luffman, the shade tree mechanic in Clinton. At the time, Tom had neither assets nor a profit and loss statement for collateral. Years later, Sewell's son, F.A., Jr., told Tom about a conversation he had with his father about the loans. He asked his father why he had loaned the money without collateral. He responded, "Son, I believe a banker has to look at the 3 C's– collateral, character, and cash flow–and while Tom Love does not have any collateral, I know his character and his cash flow is through the roof."

Fortunately for the future of Love's Country Stores, the banking environment in Oklahoma was changing dramatically just as Tom needed an infusion of cash. Globally, it was an era of hyper inflation stemming from abandonment of the gold exchange standard, the rising cost of energy, and the concentration of huge capital surpluses in the hands of totalitarian elites in oil-rich countries. In Oklahoma, while the rest of the country was suffering from an economic recession, the banking climate was overstimulated by the headlong rush into deep drilling for natural gas deposits buried several miles underground in the Deep Anadarko Basin. With interest rates exceeding twenty percent and people eager to borrow money, capital funds flowed into and through Oklahoma institutions such as the soon-to-be-famous Penn Square Bank.

One of the financial institutions growing with this transfer of capital resources into Oklahoma was Continental Federal Savings and Loan. As the oldest savings and loan in the state, founded in 1898 as the Oklahoma City Building and Loan, it plodded along slowly but steadily until the 1970s, when aggressive leaders took advantage of opportunities to grow beyond the limits of local home construction loans. In 1974, with assets climbing to more than $211 million, the name was changed to Continental Federal to reflect a new strategy of serving a statewide clientele. With his strong profit and loss statement, good cash flow, and tangible assets as collateral, Tom Love became one of those statewide clients.

While Lindell Pearson was spending the steady flow of cash from local bankers and Continental Federal to build new Country Stores, Tom and Larry were constantly looking for ways to expand the business that did not require extra square footage. What they wanted were new profit centers and strategies that would increase profits on the bottom line and be absorbed into their operating system without major disruptions or increased labor costs.

The first major change to add value to existing stores had been the expansion of operations to twenty-four hours a day, seven days a week. It was not, however, a system-wide change made overnight. At some locations, especially those in small towns where the Country Stores depended more on local customers picking up groceries than on the traveling public buying gasoline, there was little to gain with extended hours. In towns like Kingfisher and Elk City, where highway traffic was heavy and the local oil boom generated around-the-clock employment, the expanded hours made sense. The first to adopt a twenty-four-hour schedule was the Country Store in Guymon. "No one else was that crazy," remembers Fred Sledge, the local manager who had to make the schedule work. The only additional cost was adding two more hourly workers to the employee rotation, but the potential gain was a one-third increase in volume sales.

As he had done as a child, Tom associated vacations with Colorado. Here the family was on a ski trip.

The second effort to add value was a search for a line of hot fast food. The deli installed by Bill Rieck at the original service station in Watonga was not practical, because the preparation of fried chicken, smoked ribs, and fresh salads required additional labor beyond what one shift person on duty could handle at any given time. Tom and Larry wanted something that was visually appealing, tasty, and easy to prepare, but they did not want to compete with typical small town fast food franchises such as Sonic, Dairy Queen, or Pizza Hut. They wanted something unique, something that would increase foot traffic into a Love's Country Store.

In 1978, Tom and Larry found the answer after testing a proprietary concept for hot subway sandwiches in Tucson, Arizona. They came home, added a few Oklahoma twists, and announced what they called the Fresh Daily Deli. Using the Love's Country Store in Durant as a test site, Larry and his manager installed a counter-level refrigerated case just inside the front door where every customer had a good view of the deli products. Laid out were six types of sandwiches, including an Italian sub, ham and swiss, roast beef and cheddar, and turkey and swiss. Each was loaded with a generous amount of meat and cheese stacked onto the V-cut of a hoagie roll.

When a customer ordered a sandwich, the employee on duty heated it in the microwave, added dressing, and served it on a platter with chips. The beauty of the concept was in the preparation process. All the sandwiches were made on-site the previous night by the swing shift when traffic was slow. After cutting the bread and stacking the meat and cheese into the V-cut, they wrapped it to seal in the moisture and placed it in the case with the meat and cheese clearly visible. The real challenge was the bread, which had to be fresh but with a consistency that could stand up to the microwave.

The first rolls were ordered from a small family-owned bakery in Oklahoma City. The rolls worked well, but the cost of shipping every night via UPS proved to be prohibitively expensive, especially as the test sites moved farther away from the bakery. Larry tried adding ovens to twelve stores and shipping frozen dough, but he discovered baking was as much art as it was process, with precise timing and instinct required for thawing, proofing, and baking. After several attempts, they finally found a hoagie roll that could be baked by regional suppliers and delivered daily. Within a year the Fresh Daily Deli was a standard feature in all Love's Country Stores.

By the time the Love children left home for college, they had learned about the family business through experience and observation. This family portrait included (left to right) Frank, Jenny, Laura, Judy, Tom, and Greg.

By 1981, Tom Love, Larry Dillard, Lindell Pearson, Terry Ross, Harold Wells, and the rest of the Love's employee team could look back on a decade of progress. Despite gasoline shortages and changes in consumer habits, they had discovered a combination of products and services that the public wanted. Despite hyper inflation and historically low unemployment in the region, they had developed a business plan for financing, building, and staffing stores in an efficient and effective way. And despite the temptation to take profits and enjoy success, they had expanded aggressively and relentlessly reinvested in an enterprise that included more than100 Love's Country Stores scattered across the five states of Oklahoma, Kansas, Colorado, Texas, and New Mexico. They had reason to be pleased.

Tom, however, knew they could not stop. With a few exceptions, small towns in rural areas were not growing. In fact, most were shrinking as farms grew bigger, jobs grew scarce, and young people continued migrating to large towns and the jobs to be found there. And despite the shrinking markets, competition was growing as major oil companies opened self-service stations with groceries and local merchants opened look-alike convenience stores that sold self-service gasoline. In Clinton, for example, the town had four convenience stores open twenty-four hours a day by the late 1970s, including two Quick Shops, one Wag-a-Bag, and the Love's Country Store. Tom could feel his competitive advantages slipping away.

Just as he had done with the abandoned service stations in 1964 and the Country Stores in 1972, he needed to find the next opportunity. He did not have far to look.

By the 1980s, the heart was a brand associated with Love's Country Stores. Here, the image was used for door handles at the home office.

THE TRAVEL STOPS

4

Tom Love recognized that the competitive advantage of his Country Stores was coming to an end. The tight supply of gasoline, coupled with the psychological impact of the energy crisis after the Arab Oil Embargo, had given his emerging management team an opportunity to expand while others nervously waited to see if the hard times would linger. Now that the panic had vanished, both local investors and major oil companies were rushing to small towns to open their own convenience stores and self-service gas stations with extended hours of operation.

The Love family circle of leadership would come together in the 1980s and 1990s, setting the stage for a new trajectory of growth. This portrait, which appeared in the expanded Love's Country newsletter, included (from left to right) Greg, Frank, Jenny, and Tom.

There were only two limiting factors for Tom. Whatever he did, it had to be powered by growth, and that growth had to be based on family ownership.

At the same time, Tom recognized that he was armed with solid assets as he looked for new opportunities. He had a hard working team that thrived on a corporate culture that encouraged creative, independent action and kept operating costs to a bare minimum, which in turn gave him confidence that whatever direction they took, his stores could always offer the cheapest gas in town. He and his colleagues also had a deep reservoir of experience in selecting locations that catered to customers moving from place to place along a growing network of roads and highways. Just as important, with more than 100 Country Stores scattered across Oklahoma and surrounding states, his positive cash flow and tangible assets gave him flexibility to borrow investment capital.

There were only two limiting factors for Tom. Whatever he did, it had to be powered by growth, and that growth had to be based on family ownership. He was not willing to cash in on the progress already made, and he was not willing to just hold his ground. The Love's concept of cheap gas, good locations, and convenient service had to go from strength to strength, and it had to be done without relinquishing control to partners or investors. All he needed was an opportunity, a niche in the market place where an emerging demand could be satisfied with their brand of service.

In 1981, Tom and his team found that new opportunity on the interstate highway system at the very moment when the trucking industry was on the cusp of historic change.

By 1965 the miles completed across the nation doubled to 20,000 miles, which included the elevated crosstown section of I-40 through Oklahoma City and good portions of I-40 to the west and I-35 to the north.

The concept of an interstate highway system was neither new nor innovative. The Romans, two thousand years earlier, had used a system of paved roads to bind together an empire and encourage the free flow of commerce and soldiers. In 1916, and again in 1921, Congress provided matching funds and standards to encourage the states to build paved highways that accomplished the same goals. By the 1930s, while America was still building two-lane roads that surrendered safety and speed to economy and politics, Germany was lapping the rest of the world with the Autobahn, a system of limited-access super highways.

Dwight D. Eisenhower was a witness to both the limitations of the American system and the possibilities of the German experiment. In 1919, after World War I, a young Lieutenant Eisenhower participated in a coast-to-coast convoy of military troops and weapons. It took sixty-two days on the roads of that era. During World War II, as his troops rolled back the German Third Reich, he quickly recognized the advantages of the Autobahn. When he was elected President of the United States in 1952, he was ready to usher in the next generation of American highways. History was on his side.

The economy of the United States was booming, which in turn generated a growing supply of tax dollars, while the threat of Communism in Korea, China, and the expanding Soviet empire put pressure on elected officials to push back with bold action. A flush treasury and Cold War, combined with a triumphant public belief that America had not only saved the world but conquered the Great Depression, fostered an era of big dreams that included getting a man to the Moon and declaring war on poverty. In 1956, Congress responded by passing the Interstate Highway Act, the single largest public works project in world history since the great pyramids of Ancient Egypt.

The dream of a coast-to-coast interstate highway system was set in motion. The federal government, which adopted a master plan with corridors clearly defined, would provide ninety percent of the funding with ten percent provided by the states, where the work would actually be designed, contracted, and completed based on federal standards. Those standards included controlled, limited access with grades of less than three percent and curves that would be safe at seventy miles per hour. The bands of pavement would have at least four lanes plus full shoulders and at least fourteen feet of clearance under all bridges. It did not take long for the states to start spending the money and filling in the system one section at a time.

By 1960, the states had completed more than 10,000 miles of the national network. That included a good portion of I-44 in Oklahoma, with big chunks filled by the Turner Turnpike and the Will Rogers Turnpike, completed without federal assistance as toll roads in 1953 and 1957 respectively. By 1965 the miles completed across the nation doubled to 20,000 miles, which included the elevated crosstown section of I-40 through Oklahoma City and good portions of I-40 to the west and I-35 to the north. The total miles grew to 30,000 in 1970 and 40,000 miles in 1980, which largely completed the primary routes through Tom's native state along I-35, I-40, and I-44. In 1992, after thirty- five years and $425 billion invested, the last section of the national interstate highway system was completed.

The impact of interstate highways on the American landscape, like the miles of pavement laid, was incremental rather than sudden. Around cities, the interstate highways encouraged suburban sprawl with housing additions built miles from downtowns where the growing ranks of the middle class could own a home, send their children to new schools, and commute to jobs along the ribbons of pavement. In rural areas, the interstates bypassed downtown commercial districts, pulled new development to formerly vacant fields, and left in the wake a generation of underused and aging one and two-story brick buildings along Main Street.

For families raising a generation of Baby Boomers, the interstates made long distance travel more efficient, if less interesting. Vacations to Disneyland, Yellowstone, or Padre Island no longer were adventures filled with diners, alligator farms, and dangerous

The Interstate Highway system, authorized by Congress in 1956, created a new market for bigger and better travel stops that quickly replaced the traditional mom and pop truck stops. Tom Love eagerly seized the opportunity. (*Courtesy ODOT.*)

The shift from travel-by-railroad to travel-by-car after World War II was reflected in a new generation of lodging located on the new interstate highway system. Holiday Inn was an industry leader in replacing the traditional downtown hotels located near railroad depots.

two-lane bridges, but rather long bouts of marathon driving to get from one well known attraction to another. Enterprising merchants filled those seemingly endless "are we there yet" miles with the twenty-eight flavors of Howard Johnson's ice cream, the pecan logs at Stuckey's candy stores, and the uninspired but consistently clean rooms at Holiday Inn motels.

The interstate highway system accelerated what had been a slow transition from railroads to trucks as a means of moving freight. Beginning in the 1930s, trucks enjoyed flexibility and price advantages over railroads, but that had been minimized partly by the extra time, limited capacity, and potential danger of hauling heavy loads over the narrow and winding two lane roads that stretched across the countryside like a spider's web. Trains were dependable, capable of carrying heavy loads, and owned by railroad corporations that were politically well connected and protective of their customer base.

In 1935, Congress responded to the political demands of the railroad industry by passing the first federal Motor Carrier Act to

What Holiday Inn did for a new age of lodging, Howard Johnson's was doing for road food. Instead of local cafes in small towns, travelers looked for consistency and convenience on the side of the highway.

regulate interstate trucking and suppress what railroad officials termed "destructive competition." The means for accomplishing that goal included a permitting process, which limited access to the roads, controlled monopolies, and a fare-making system that allowed trucking cartels to set rates with exemption from anti-trust laws. The result was limited competition, high costs for shipping by truck, and lack of innovation in an industry that was protected from change. That protected status was under assault by the 1970s, just as the interstate highway system was coming together to offer greater efficiencies with heavier loads. The renewed political battle, ironically, was not a fight between railroaders and truckers, but a fight to tame the inferno of runaway inflation. The fuel for that fire, as mentioned already, came from monetary adjustments to abandonment of the gold exchange standard, long standing manipulation of the free market economy through price controls, and the rising cost of energy following the Arab Oil Embargo. President Jimmy Carter, along with a majority of the members of Congress, used the tools of deregulation to ease controls that sheltered companies from market pressures.

First came the Airline Deregulation Act of 1978, which unchained start-up aviation companies like Southwest and JetBlue and allowed them to take on entrenched major carriers like Pan Am, TWA, and Eastern. The result was increased competition and lower fares. Then came the Motor Carrier Act of 1980, landmark legislation affecting the trucking industry that encouraged independent pricing, opened access to routes for anyone willing to take a risk, and eliminated most restrictions on commodities that could be carried. Before the act was passed, truck companies had used controlled monopolies to simply pass along higher wages and bloated operating costs to shippers, who in turn passed the costs along to consumers. After the act, the trucking industry playing field was open to anyone hungry enough and clever enough to reduce costs and deliver quality service.

As implemented during the administration of President Ronald Reagan, the Motor Carrier Act of 1980 revolutionized the trucking industry. Despite a dramatic reduction in shipping rates, the number of licensed carriers exploded from 18,000 in 1980 to 49,000 in 1992. Most were either owner-operators, who owned their truck but leased their services to a major company, or independent owner-operators, who not only owned their trucks but also retained the authority to ship for anybody anywhere. Most of this latter group had from one to ten trucks in their start-up companies and most used the growing interstate highway system to get goods from one point to another as quickly and cheaply as possible.

Enterprising merchants filled those seemingly endless "are we there yet" miles with the twenty-eight flavors of Howard Johnson's ice cream, the pecan logs at Stuckey's candy stores, and the uninspired but consistently clean rooms at Holiday Inn motels.

The exploding number of owner-operator trucks on interstate corridors, armed with the authority to buy diesel anywhere they could get a good deal, created an opportunity for enterprising fuel merchants. Long established local truck stops, some of which had grown soft and seedy during the decades of limited competition, were absorbed by corporate giants with dreams of a national footprint. One of the first to make that move was the Union Oil Company of California, better known as Unocal.

As early as the 1930s, Unocal was a fully integrated oil company that operated a string of service stations under the brand of Union 76. While making money in exploration, production, refining, and retail distribution, the company accumulated large real estate holdings in Southern California. When the interstate highway system was launched, Unocal was one of the first major oil companies to see the value of real estate at key points of the system and the potential of truck stops with a national reach. The Union 76 brand had a huge head start on regional competitors.

One of the newcomers fighting for a share of that market was Truckstops of America, founded in 1972 by Phil Saunders in Ohio. Saunders would grow his company over the next four decades through consolidation with other corporate chains. In 1997, he

Love's Travel Stops was one of many regional start-ups trying to tap the growing market of car and truck travel on interstate highways. One of the most aggressive was Flying J, based in the northern Rocky Mountain region.

acquired Union 76 and changed the name of the combined companies to TravelCenters of America, with a brand of TA. Then he purchased Petro, a truck stop chain started in 1975 by Jack Cardwell in El Paso, Texas. By the time the combined company was taken over by a Wall Street investment trust in 2006, it was using both names, TravelCenters of America (TA) and Petro.

Equally dependent on corporate partners and consolidation were several regional companies with roots in full-service gasoline stations. One was Pilot, incorporated by Jim Haslam, who had opened his first service station in Gate City, Virginia, in 1958. Seven years later, struggling with debt, Haslam sold half of his company to Marathon Oil, which provided the funds to build a string of convenience stores and his first travel center in 1981 on the interstate highway system at Corbin, Kentucky. Haslam's sons, Jimmy and Bill, would eventually expand the chain of corporate truck stops from their base in Tennessee.

A similar path of growth through consolidation and mergers with oil companies was taken by O. Jay Call, who bought his first service station in Idaho in 1964. By 1968, with four stations, he organized the Flying J Corporation and started expanding. Call opened his first truck stop in 1979 near West Haven, Utah, and quickly followed that with the purchases of a Canadian oil company with refineries in North Dakota and Montana and Husky Oil Company that included refineries, pipelines, and an additional forty service stations and truck stops. Flying J's base of expansion would be from the intermountain region of the American Northwest.

There was another company, this one located in the American Southwest, ready to tap the growing market for diesel fuel sales to truckers along the expanding interstate highway system. But unlike its onrushing competitors, this company was family owned and dedicated to steady growth, one step at a time, without giving up control to oil companies or compromising the core values on which it was built.

That company was Love's Country Stores.

Even before deregulation of trucking, Tom Love had recognized the coming impact of the new interstate highways. It was affecting his chain of Love's Country Stores, many of which were located on the old generation of two-lane interstates, such as Route 66, U.S. Highway 81, and U.S. Highway 77. With his finger on the pulse of traffic flow, mix of resident and tourist customers, and the ebb and flow of fuel sales, he felt the tidal wave of change coming his way.

Tom and his team of managers had a rough idea of where they wanted to go with their next phase of growth. They needed an emerging market where they could get ahead of competitors and gain an advantage that would sustain them when they faced the inevitable market pressure. Just as important, due to the shrinking profit margin in the sale of gasoline after the Arab Oil Embargo, they needed more volume to maintain the strong cash flow that had been the foundation of the Love's business model since 1964. If they made less on each gallon of gasoline, they needed to sell more gallons.

They also needed to add more profit centers, just as they had done when they added groceries to the service stations and deli food to the Country Stores. At the same time, they needed to keep operational costs at the bare minimum in order to maintain the never-changing cornerstone of their enterprise, the ability to offer the cheapest fuel in town. Sensing that he could find that combination of advantages along the emerging interstate highway system, Tom started investigating the possibilities.

In 1980, with diesel fuel sales to truckers as the potential new profit center, Tom and Terry Ross started assembling clues to find the right combination of what would work for them. Each would hit the road, usually on the way to visit a Country Store or check out a potential new location, and stop at existing truck stops to observe what worked and why it worked. They had an easel in Terry's office where they listed information about size of lots, layouts of buildings, number and location of pumps, staffing numbers, size and quantity of products, and the systems used to sell diesel. Within a year, they had a good idea of what they wanted.

Essentially, they would build a Country Store on steroids with a bigger building, a larger inventory of merchandise, and a more ambitious Fresh Daily Deli. They would keep and expand the number of gasoline pumps to retain their traditional customer base of people driving cars both locally and cross-country. They would order products such as oil in gallons and cases rather than cans. The big difference would be the addition of diesel islands separate from the gasoline pumps with enough real estate to allow for convenient and safe turning lanes needed by eighteen-wheelers.

Just as important, they decided what they would not do in the new stores. They would not add showers, drivers' lounges with televisions, or large parking lots where truckers could stay overnight. Each added to the cost of delivering a gallon of diesel to a customer, which would force them to either squeeze the already thin profit margin or raise prices, and each would require more capital invest-

> Essentially, they would build a Country Store on steroids with a bigger building, a larger inventory of merchandise, and a more ambitious Fresh Daily Deli.

Although the travel stops offered the greatest potential for aggressive growth in the 1980s, the Love's leadership team continued to improve the smaller but profitable Country Stores with new merchandise, operational efficiencies, and the ever-present "cheapest gas in town."

dimensional multi-tasking and steely nerves. The person on the fuel desk stood in front of a switchboard with a view of the diesel pump islands. After arriving, the trucker pressed a button on the intercom to give the clerk a long list of information that included name, truck company, payment method, and amount of fuel needed. If the truck driver was using a credit card or proprietary payment system, the clerk had to call the credit service, provide all the information, and wait for confirmation. All of that was written by hand on an invoice. Once confirmed, the pumps were activated and the driver filled his tanks before coming into the store and signing the invoice or paying in cash. There could be up to eight transactions underway at any given time.

As a veteran of Love's Country Stores, Dan Sena already knew the duties of a store manager, which included daily paperwork to track inventories, total sales, and count cash for deposit. More important was the responsibility of hiring a staff and nurturing a culture of team work that matched store appearance with customer service. All of the team members were expected to do whatever was necessary, from working one of three registers and restocking shelves to preparing food at the deli and cleaning the bathrooms. At all times they were encouraged to do so with a smile and friendliness for the customer. Although the maintenance man handled most of the demanding duties around the site, it was common for a manager or hourly worker to buff floors or use the steam-cleaning power washer on the diesel pumps.

Terry Ross still remembers the opening on the Monday following Easter Sunday in 1981. "We were amazed with the volume of traffic that first day...we had a steady stream of trucks buying diesel, which did not seem to impact the willingness of customers in cars from coming in and shopping for both gasoline and merchandise." Most memorable was the shock that first night. "I will never forget counting cash before I left that evening," Terry recalls. "I was stacking so many $100 bills that I started to get nervous thinking about the drive to the bank for the daily deposit...before I left town, we hired an armored car service to come by every day to pick up deposits." What they had not anticipated were the large bills carried by truck owner-operators who had no credit.

The overnight success of the first Love's in Amarillo fanned the flames of Tom's natural appetite for expansion, just as Oklahoma and much of the American Southwest was experiencing an economic boom of epic proportions. The boom was based on the rush to drill for and produce natural gas, especially from the prolific deep Anadarko Basin in western Oklahoma. With federal regulation keeping the price of "old gas" below the cost of finding and producing it, the deregulation of price controls on "new gas" sent prices soaring. Along with the flow of capital investment that swelled the coffers of regional banks came an attitude that anything was possible if only a person was willing to take a chance. There was even a commercial on television in Oklahoma City that showed a beautiful model on a drilling rig saying, "If you don't own an oil well, get one."

Tom did not need encouragement to take a risk. Even before the Amarillo store opened, he and his team had been looking for additional sites along the interstate highway system. They found one near Pauls Valley, south of Oklahoma City on I-35, where they opened the second Love's in August of 1981. Then came in quick succession stores on I-40 on the west edge of Oklahoma City and on I-25 near Longmont, Colorado. In each case, banks with growing deposits were eager to find customers willing to invest their funds. Then came a couple of speed bumps on the road to expansion.

After the store north of Denver opened in the spring of 1982, Tom received a letter from attorneys in Los Angeles claiming trademark infringement. There was a company in Southern California called Love's Wood Pit Barbeque owned by Brian Padbur, who had worked for Ray Kroc when McDonald's was expanding through franchising in the 1970s. Padbur intended to do the same with the Love's restaurants, and when his field representative was in Colorado looking for potential franchisees, he saw the Love's Travel Stop on I-25 and reported it to his boss, who in turn had his attorneys send the letter to Tom

As with other challenges in the past, Tom turned the problem into an asset. He had already hired a marketing firm in New York to work on a new branding image with colors and graphics that would help pull customers off interstate highways. The firm was

Lister-Butler, founded in 1977 and led by John Lister, who believed that a brand was a promise that distinguished one company from its competitors. Lister-Butler's client list would eventually include Kodak, Kraft Foods, PepsiCo, 3M, British Petroleum, and AT&T. At the time, Tom thought their fees were "absolutely unfathomable," but he eventually changed his mind.

Lister and his team recommended both a graphics package and a solution for the trademark problem. For the store facades and signs, they chose distinctive shades of yellow, red, and brown that were highly visible from great distances. The colors were used in horizontal bands around the stores and canopies over the pumps, on the signs, and eventually on products and trucks. For signage, they recommended a Paddington block lettering, which was easy to read and replaced the cursive lettering on the old Love's Country Store signs. Finishing touches were the repeating echo hearts and the little red heart used for the apostrophe in Love's. When Tom offered to drop the cursive letters, which he was going to do anyway, the restaurant chain dropped their trademark infringement lawsuit. "It was one of the smartest investments we ever made," Tom would recall almost thirty years later.

While the Love's team dealt with the trademark battle, the aggressive plans for expansion bumped up against a collapsing economy in Oklahoma and the Southwest. President Ronald Reagan, with his first executive order, deregulated all natural gas price controls, just as oil and gas companies were finding and producing a growing supply of natural gas. By the summer of 1982, with the market forces of supply and demand running headlong into the turbulence of sudden deregulation, the price of oil and gas plunged, and with it, companies went bankrupt and banks failed. The loudest crash was the fall of Penn Square Bank in Oklahoma

The graphics package on signage changed from script (facing page) to block (left) as part of a trademark dispute with a barbeque chain in California. The new sign included a heart as the apostrophe.

The infamous failure of Penn Square Bank in 1982 started a chain of banking failures in Oklahoma that affected businesses such as Love's that depended on rapid growth. Refusing to back down, Tom and his team turned to other methods of raising cash for expansion.

City on July 5, 1982, followed by the closing of sixty-nine banks in the state of Oklahoma over the next seven years. The biggest failure was the First National Bank of Oklahoma City, once known as the entrepreneurial bank of the Southwest. By 1985 the boom had turned to bust.

Tom and the Love's team felt the pain, especially in their ability to borrow money to fuel expansion. With Oklahoma locked in its second Great Depression and profit margins tightening, they had to find other ways to increase cash flow and keep the momentum going forward. Watching competitors on all sides rushing to catch up, they could not stand still.

Tom knew there were two ways to grow. One was to add more stores, which was his North Star. At the same time, he knew that external expansion with new locations had to be balanced with increases in same store sales and something other than the cheapest gasoline and diesel fuel. Just as the Fresh Daily Deli had added another profit center and branding tool for the Country Stores, he and Larry Dillard wanted products and services that set them apart from the competition. They needed something unique, something that would appeal to both truckers and tourists. They found it in an unlikely but familiar place, Love County, Oklahoma, named in honor of Tom's Chickasaw ancestors.

The vendor was V.B. "Tup" Robertson, an enterprising cowboy who returned home from World War II and built a combination frozen food locker plant, grocery store, and feed store in his hometown of Marietta, Oklahoma. By 1959, along with anything to make a living, he and his brothers were selling smoked meats from a small stand on U.S. Highway 77. They could smoke fifteen hams at a time. Within a decade they had franchised stores and a selection of smoked meats that included beef jerky slow cooked over hickory. The only problem was the small cut of beef with the right grain and texture needed for Robertson's jerky.

Tom and Larry went to see Tup to talk about jerky. They learned that good jerky could not be made from a prime cut of beef or it was too rich and would not cure properly. If it was too lean, the jerky dried out before it absorbed the smoke flavor. They took a look at the plant and talked about the possibility of buying large quantities to be packaged and sold in Love's Country Stores and Travel Stops. When Tup asked Tom how much he wanted to buy, Tom said, "all of it." Within a year, Love's Beef Jerky by Robertson's Hams was being sold in every store and earning a devoted following of repeat customers.

While the never-ending search for new products and greater efficiencies continued, Tom knew that the quicker way to grow was adding more stores to the system, especially if a way could be found to reduce the costs of initial investment in the face of tight money supplies. In 1985, just as the economy was reaching its deepest point of depression, a timely opportunity presented itself. Tom would remember it as the Stuckey's deal.

Stuckey's was an iconic American company founded in the 1930s by W.S. Stuckey, a pecan farmer in Georgia who found a way to market surplus pecans by converting them to pecan candies created by his wife, Ethel. Her specialties, as any sweet-toothed Baby Boomer knows, were pecan logs and pecan divinity. Stuckey opened his first road-side lean-to in 1937, then added a restaurant, novelty section, and finally gas pumps. By 1960, there were more than 350 of his distinctive buildings with teal-blue roofs scattered from coast to coast.

In 1967, just as competition on the emerging interstate highway system was on the verge of offering greater variety and forcing merchants to lower their operating costs, Stuckey's was purchased by Pet Milk. More corporate and less personal, management of the chain stopped innovating and watched the competition gradually take its market share. In 1979, two years after the death of the founder, Pet Milk sold the chain of stores to IC Industries, which started liquidating the stores for the value of the real estate. By 1985, when the Stuckey family repurchased the brand, only eighty of the 350 Stuckey's were still operating.

In this one bold move, when others were pulling back under the force of the failing economy, Tom picked up key real estate and doubled the number of branded stores on the interstate highway system.

While coping with the credit crisis, Tom could not resist the opportunity to buy twenty-five aging Stuckey's stores in Arkansas and Texas. In one bold move, he doubled Love's presence on the interstate highway system.
(Flickr Creative Commons Credit: LonghornDave)

Tom Love, despite the pressures of declining same-store sales and a banking crisis in his home state, seized the chance to buy twenty-five of the Stuckey's. He paid $4.8 million for nineteen stores in Texas and $1.2 million for six stores in Arkansas. What he really bought was the land at each site, with the buildings, tanks, and infrastructure thrown in for good measure. An added bonus was the fact that the land would serve as collateral for loans. Considering the fact that within a few decades even one site on the interstate system might cost millions, the Stuckey's deal was a bargain.

Instead of tearing down the buildings and borrowing even more money for new construction, the Love's team remodeled the old Stuckey's stores and added diesel bays and paving for trucks. The remodeling generally consisted of upgrading the bathrooms, converting the old grills to deli counters, and retrofitting the exterior with the colors and signage of a rebranded Love's. In this one bold move, when others were pulling back under the force of the failing economy, Tom picked up key real estate and doubled the number of branded stores on the interstate highway system.

While part of his management team pressed on trying to open new Love's despite the difficult economy, Tom turned his passion for growth to a completely new business model that for the first time did not include the sale of fuel. The initial experiment, prompted by an innovative new technology just on the market, was a full- service, brushless car wash called AutoGraf. The first car wash owned by the Love family opened in Oklahoma City at N. May and Hefner in 1985, followed by a second location in Tulsa at 71st and Sheridan.

The roof line of this Love's store reveals its previous identity as a Stuckey's. The Love's sign with the distinctive heart on top and the proud display of the lowest-cost fuel in the market set it apart from the location's troubled past.

Each car wash, offering full detail and hand rubbed drying, employed up to twenty-five people at times, especially in the winter when the weather cleared and it was too cold for people to wash their own cars. The problem was the seasonal nature of the business. It was either feast or famine, which made it difficult to balance manpower and demand. Although both car washes were sold within ten years, the experience convinced managers to add smaller, less labor intensive car washes at existing stores in the 1990s.

This urge to take a risk and look for new opportunities continued well into the early 1990s as managers searched for ways to return same-store profitability to the levels achieved in the early 1980s before the crash in the oil patch. "You have to create the sort of atmosphere so that employees know you appreciate what they do and that that you listen to them," Tom told a reporter at the time. "When someone comes up with an idea, we discuss it and if it seems like it might work, the person that thought of it gets to head it. They seem to like that."

As if reflecting this willingness to depart from the past, the Love family changed the corporate name in September of 1990 to Love's Country Stores, Inc. Musket Corporation, the entity created by Tom and Judy in 1964, would survive as a wholesale fuel company buying and distributing gasoline and diesel not only to company stores, but also to other customers in their trade territory. Hopefully, that group led by Vice President Terry Ross would create a new profit center and lower costs at individual stores.

After serving as Tom's field general of operations for almost twenty years, Larry Dillard retired in 1991.

Another departure from the past was the retirement of Larry Dillard in August of 1991. For almost twenty years, while Tom and his development team had focused on expansion, Larry had run the operational side of the growing company. When he stepped down, there were eighty-seven Country Stores and thirty-nine Travel Stops. In a letter to all store employees, Tom wrote, "The accomplishments of the past decades include financial and operating progress...we are proud of our past accomplishments and Larry Dillard has played a critical role in that success."

In the wake of that major change, Tom announced his new leadership team. For the vice president of operations, he promoted Bill Spence, who had been with Love's for approximately six years, two of those as vice president of human resources. Terry Ross also assumed expanded duties with strategic planning, special projects, and new store marketing concepts added to retail and wholesale fuel operations. The chief financial officer was Paula Downing, who had come to Love's as head of accounting from a similar position at Braum's Dairy and Ice Cream Stores, a regional company in Oklahoma. There was one other critical position on the leadership team that needed to be filled. It was vice president of real estate and construction, once held by Lindell Pearson who had since retired. The new man in that key leadership role was Greg Love, Tom and Judy's oldest son.

Greg had literally grown up in the business. As a young man, he remembered talking to his father about locations and traffic counts while on spring break vacations. During summer vacations from Bishop McGuinness High School, he worked as an hourly employee at a Country Store located at 2nd Street and Santa Fe Avenue west of Edmond. Construction workers building the new Oak Tree Country Club were some of his best customers.

His range of experience with the company expanded during summers while attending Trinity University in San Antonio. In 1981, he spent two months working at the new truck stop in Amarillo, followed by three weeks at the new truck stop in Elk City. Later, he gained additional operational experience as an assistant manager at the Travel Stop in El Paso, Texas. While in college, he shadowed Lindell Pearson for three summers as they traveled around the country searching for new locations and working with contractors to build new stores. When Greg graduated from college with experience in both operations and site evaluation, he was made manager of the new AutoGraf Car Wash in Tulsa, a position he held for almost two years.

In 1986, just as the Stuckey's deal was about to double the size of the company, Greg was pulled into the central office to work with contractors renovating the old roadside candy stores. It was like a military field promotion with the battle raging on all fronts. Some of the assumptions made during the acquisition phase did not work as planned, and costs were spiraling upward as some in the company questioned their decision to buy the aging stores. Septic systems in some places did not work. Sites were too small at others. Some stores were in the wrong place. Greg had to sort the good from the bad, plan a way to deal with the problems, and take advantage of the opportunities.

As the field general executing the Stuckey's plan, Greg completed a crash course in site evaluation, a process he later described as a combination of science and art. He learned to interpret data from traffic counts and sales reports. He developed a keen eye for subtle details that ranged from sight lines and setbacks to lot layouts and proximity of competitors. He noticed that the distance from cities made a difference in both the volume and mix of customers. By the time the company had all twenty-five of the Stuckey's stores converted to Love's, Greg had the confidence needed to pull the trigger on the one decision that could not be improved once it was made. That decision was where to build the next Love's.

In 1987, Greg began his first independent search for a new location with two principle goals. One, based on the Stuckey's expe-

After summers working at Love's stores and graduating from college, Greg Love (above) earned the chance to start a new enterprise called the AutoGraf Car Wash (below). Although it did not fit the operational model of Love's, managing the store gave Greg valuable experience he later applied to his position as president of the company.

rience, he knew that up to seventy-five percent of gross sales would be to drivers in cars, many of whom were traveling long distances with families. The other was the belief that sixty miles from the nearest large city was the best location where families would most likely need to stop, not just for gasoline, but also for a bathroom break, snacks, and souvenirs. And it was important to be sixty miles from the city on the side of the highway leading away, not into town. For a family going on vacation, getting out of town was the first anxious step to fun, and by the time they were on the road they were relaxed enough to stop for that full tank of gasoline and a few treats with a pocket full of cash set aside for the trip.

Greg found that first location sixty miles east of Oklahoma City on I-40 at the Seminole exit on U.S. Highway 99. The intersection was in a rural area, with good visibility from the highway and only one small convenience store and a Robertson's Hams outlet. Greg bought thirty-three acres for $65,000, and it was on the south side of the highway leading out of Oklahoma City. The Love's team then built a 4,000-square-foot building, four gas pumps that could serve eight cars at a time, and three diesel bays where six trucks could be fueled simultaneously. By the time that Love's opened, the company had $3 million invested.

One downside to locating new Love's stores in rural areas, especially at the pace Tom wanted, was the difficulty in securing loans for the initial investment. The most common source of loans had long been local bankers who wanted to see development in their towns, but in rural areas, that connection was missing. The other source of money for expansion had been Continental Federal Savings and Loan and other big banks in Oklahoma City. Continental failed in 1988 and the survivors were cash strapped and much more conservative as weak banks succumbed to the economic crisis in the oil patch and bank regulators tightened guidelines for lending.

In the late 1980s and early 1990s, Tom found another source of cash for the growth he craved. It was called a lease-back. Paula Downing, his chief financial officer, had experience with lease-backs at Braum's Dairy Stores, her previous employer. Other companies weened on growth, such as QuikTrip based in Tulsa, used the same financial tool. Simplified, the lease-back started by selling a developed property to a third party, who in turn leased it back to the developer as a monthly rental over a specified period of time. The cash funded subsequent expansion, while the high cash flow at a Love's covered the rental payments. Although more expensive than conventional bank loans, it fueled the fire for growth when there were few options.

> By the time the company had all twenty-five of the Stuckey's stores converted to Love's, Greg had the confidence needed to pull the trigger on the one decision that could not be improved once it was made. That decision was where to build the next Love's.

The willingness to try new strategies and experiment with variations on fundamental practices increased during the early 1990s as the company was still struggling with stale same-store sales and tight profit margins. One of the most daring was an ambitious project called the Oklahoma Trading Post, a free-standing gift shop built in 1992 adjacent to a Love's Travel Stop on I-40 just west of the Oklahoma-Arkansas border near Webbers Falls.

The experiment with products other than groceries and snacks had started in a small way in the mid-1980s as the Love's Travel Stops grew progressively larger with each new store. By 1985, Larry Dillard's buyers were adding items that appealed to truckers, such as hats, jackets, shirts, and gloves. Then came the Stuckey's deal, with new insights into what tourists wanted in the way of high profit souvenirs and t-shirts. The Trading Post took that incremental tinkering to a new, more aggressive level.

The building itself was a radical departure from the past. The rough-cedar false front, broad front porch with rocking chairs, and gift items reflecting the spirit of the Southwest were aimed at tourists. With the stated goal that the stores "would help us discover new successful gift items which we can put in the Travel Stops and Convenience Stores," the Love's team built two more Trading Posts, one on the north edge of Oklahoma City at N.W. 122nd and I-35 and the other near Amarillo on I-40. The latter was called the Texas Trading Post.

In this newfound spirit of experimentation, Tom and his evolving management team turned their attention to another profit center that had not progressed beyond initial success. That new frontier was food.

By the 1990s, there were two growing market segments for road food served along the interstate highway system. One was fast food, delivered under a rainbow of chains from McDonald's and Wendy's to Burger King and Taco Bell. There was another, smaller market for home-cooked meals that cost a little more and took a little longer to serve and eat. One of the leading innovators in this field was Dan Evins, who opened his first Cracker Barrel in 1969 on I-40 near Lebanon, Tennessee. By 1990, there were eighty-four Cracker Barrels on the interstate system serving what Evins called "honest country food" in a down-home, rustic setting with fire places, checker boards, and a gift shop customers had to navigate before getting to the food.

After experimenting with a free-standing Grandy's next to a Loves Travel Stop at I-40 and Morgan Road in Oklahoma City, the

Another Love's experiment outside the industry of fuel distribution was inspired by the early success of upscale road food offered with a gauntlet of merchandise between the front door and the dining room.

Love's management team developed their own version of a full service restaurant with regional flair. They called it Cowboy's. The site for the innovative prototype was a lot next to the Love's Travel Stop on I-40 in far western Oklahoma near Erick, the hometown of Roger Miller, the talented musician and comedian who fittingly wrote the hit song, "King of the Road." On February 11, 1992, ground was broken for a 7,000-square-foot, western-style building with 2,500 square feet set aside for a gift shop and 4,500 square feet for a restaurant and seating for 146 people.

The theme of Cowboy's was "A Tradition of Great Southwestern Cooking." The menu, with items such as "Whistle Wett'in Drinks," "Saddle Sides," "Chuck Wagon Pancakes," and "Trail Boss Steak and Eggs," was illustrated with drawings of cowboy life and culture described in historic terms with stories from the Old West. Greeting guests as they entered the false-front building was a seventeen-foot-tall wooden sculpture of a cowboy carved from an

Love's version of upscale road food with merchandise was called Cowboy's Restaurant & Trading Post. Like the car wash, the business model did not blend well with Love's operations, but it did provide valuable experience as the Love's team started adding food outlets in their stores. Cowboy's also lured Jenny (facing page) back to Oklahoma and a place in the management team.

8,000-pound Western Red Cedar. It required a staff of about fifty people to run the restaurant and gift shop. One of those staff members was a young lady named Jenny Love.

Like her older brother, Jenny grew up in the business. As a child, she watched her father take time to visit each store on every trip they took so he could talk to the employees. "He taught us that the employees make the business go," she remembered years later. "I saw the reaction to my father when he walked into their stores," she added. "Their faces lit up...he was like a rock star." That personal connection between the Love family and team members at the stores would leave an indelible imprint on Jenny's memory.

During one summer break from Colorado College, where she majored in political science and spent as much time as possible on the ski slopes, Jenny saw Love's stores from a different perspective. She and her cousin, Kevin McCarthy, installed VeriFone credit card reading machines in Country Stores spread across Western Oklahoma. Years later, she would remember one trip to Hooker, Oklahoma, where they circled around to surrounding stores meeting managers and team members.

In 1988, after graduating from college, Jenny found a job in Washington, D.C. at the Bellevue Hotel near Capitol Hill. She worked in reservations the first year, then moved up to manager of the restaurant, which she later described as primarily a big bar that happened to sell food. For another year and a half she managed a large and diverse staff, which was unionized, and learned the basics of food service from inventory control and customer relationships to cash management and quality control. Most of all, she learned that she had a talent for working with people. "It was a tremendous lesson for me," she would later recall, "in terms of managing people and getting the desired results through teamwork."

In 1991, as planning for Cowboy's Restaurant was moving ahead, Tom told Jenny he needed her to be his eyes and ears and use her expertise in food service as they developed and launched the concept. The challenge sounded intriguing, so she moved back to Oklahoma and joined the team of Jim Parsons, food service director for Love's, Kevin Asbury, district manager for Western Oklahoma and the Texas Panhandle, and Rob Muncrief, manager of the Love's Travel Stop next door to Cowboy's. Jenny represented the family at the ground breaking.

For a year and a half, the restaurant manager and his staff moved from a concept to a work-in-progress. Although the food and service met their expectations, the number of customers taking a seat in the restaurant did not. The customer count was good in

"I saw the reaction to my father when he walked into their stores. Their faces lit up...he was like a rock star." The personal connection between the Love family and team members at the stores would leave an indelible imprint on Jenny's memory.

the summer when families were on vacation, but in the winter it dropped dramatically. As it turned out, full-service themed restaurants such as Cowboys and Cracker Barrel had to be in or near big cities in order to have both a visitor and resident clientele. Tourists and truck drivers alone were not enough.

The experiment convinced the Love's management team that quick-service food was the better bet for their locations. What they needed, it was decided, was a smaller version of a fast food restaurant that had a national brand. From the standpoint of efficiency, it needed to be inside existing buildings, which limited the initial capital investment, and it needed to fit into the space previously used for the Fresh Daily Deli, which utilized existing staffing levels and provided a strategic location highly visible to customers. Most importantly, the national branding needed to attract the attention of cross-country travelers who might otherwise not be familiar with a Love's Travel Stop. In 1993 the Love's management team launched their first experiment in this new market. It was called a Taco Bell Express.

Adding restaurants to Love's Travel Stops accomplished several goals. Hopefully, they not only made money, but also gave travelers another reason to stop at a Love's rather than a competitor's store and created a new career path to recruit and retain hourly workers.

Glen Bell, a native of Southern California where car culture had first merged with recreational eating to create something called a drive-in, opened his first Taco Bell in 1962. Two years later he sold his first franchise, and by the time PepsiCo bought the company in 1978, Taco Bells were scattered across the country with an aggressive marketing campaign on television that made it one of the most recognizable names in the food industry. In 1991, targeting convenience stores, shopping malls, and truck stops, the company opened its first Taco Bell Express, a small version of the restaurant with a limited menu, items generally priced under one dollar, and a business plan that relied more on volume sales than high profit margin. The first Taco Bell Express was in San Francisco.

The first Taco Bell Express in a Love's was opened at the Travel Stop at I-240 and Sooner Road in Oklahoma City. As a licensee, rather than a franchisee, Love's did not pay for territorial rights or training and support. What they were buying was the name, the recipes and cooking processes, and the rights to use all logos and signage at a Love's. While this gave the Love's team greater flexibility in making the concept work within their existing buildings and operations, it required more adaptive innovation and creativity.

One of the most important considerations was keeping operational costs as low as possible. As with the Fresh Daily Deli, one person was assigned to the Express line each shift, with additional help provided by the assistant manager or manager when needed. No additional supervisors were needed, while the pay scales and employee rules were the same as for other employees. Even though the line worker might wear a Taco Bell Express uniform, he or she was part of the shift team and subject to doing whatever was needed at any given time.

As the Love's team opened additional Taco Bell Expresses in Oklahoma, Texas, Arkansas, Louisiana, and New Mexico, they recognized limitations on where the concept would work. Because they were serving hot food that had a short shelf life, they needed a high volume of customers to avoid excessive waste. They put lines in a few Country Stores, but generally it worked better in the Travel Stops where the customer turnover was greater. The experiment reached forty-two locations by 1997, when Taco Bell started requiring drive-in windows for their Express licensees. The Express had worked well, but they could not adapt all of their stores to the drive-in windows. By that time, the Love's management team had found another quick service restaurant that fit their needs even better. It was called SUBWAY.

A teenager named Fred DeLuca had sold his first submarine sandwich in 1965 from a shop in Connecticut. Three years later, after adding a partner and additional stores, he started using the name SUBWAY. By 1974, they were selling franchises that featured fresh baked bread, an efficient preparation line that minimized labor, and a brand that combined the image of the New York City subway system with healthy choices in a marketplace dominated by hamburger chains. By the 1990s, SUBWAY had a national brand with heavy advertising on television.

Love's became a corporate franchisee, which included territorial rights wherever a SUBWAY was added. Another advantage was a reduction in waste. Like the old Fresh Daily Deli, the bread was kept fresh after baking and the food was kept cold throughout a shift. Any heating was done only after an order was taken. And like the Taco Bell Express, the branding achieved its purpose every time the SUBWAY sign on the highway convinced a traveler to stop at a Love's instead of a competitor. In most cases, the stop turned into another tank of gasoline sold. By 1997, there were nineteen SUBWAYS in Love's Travel Stops.

This experiment with quick service restaurants included other brands as well. The Love's team wanted a hamburger franchise, but they bumped up against the territorial rights already held by franchisees of nationally advertised chains such as McDonald's, Burger King, and Wendy's. They turned instead to A&W, known for their root beer and one of the oldest franchises in the business that dated to the 1930s in Southern California. From 1993 to 1997, fourteen A&Ws were added to the Love's system. Other franchises tried in a few sites included Pizza Hut and Baskin-Robbins. By 1997, there were sixty-two branded foods in forty-five Love's Travel Stops and Country Stores. And that was just the beginning.

Like the Love's Fresh Daily Deli sandwich counters in the 1970s, SUBWAY provided efficient road food with little waste but added another marketing brand to pull customers off the interstate highways.

By 1997, all of the moving parts of a profitable regional company selling a combination of fuel and merchandise were in place. Fuel sales drove cash flow and pulled customers off the interstate highways and into stores where they bought food, groceries, and a growing inventory of specialty items. Low operating costs protected profit margins. And the constant expansion of new stores not only created a sense of urgency, but also fostered a culture of creativity and hard-working teamwork. By all standards, Love's was a profitable, successful enterprise.

Tom Love thought they could do better.

What he saw was a work in progress, with a fundamental business plan that was adaptable, a regional base from which they could expand from coast to coast, and a work ethic shared by a team of managers and front line workers that gave him confidence to push even harder. He also saw the challenges. They were bumping up against other regional giants on all sides as they expanded, which put pressure on profit margins and exposed his best workers to competitors who lured them away with higher pay and greater benefits. More seriously, they were constantly outrunning their internal ability to turn the moving parts of the enterprise into a smoothly working machine.

Through hard work and perseverance, they had come far. To keep the momentum, they needed to take their operations to a higher level.

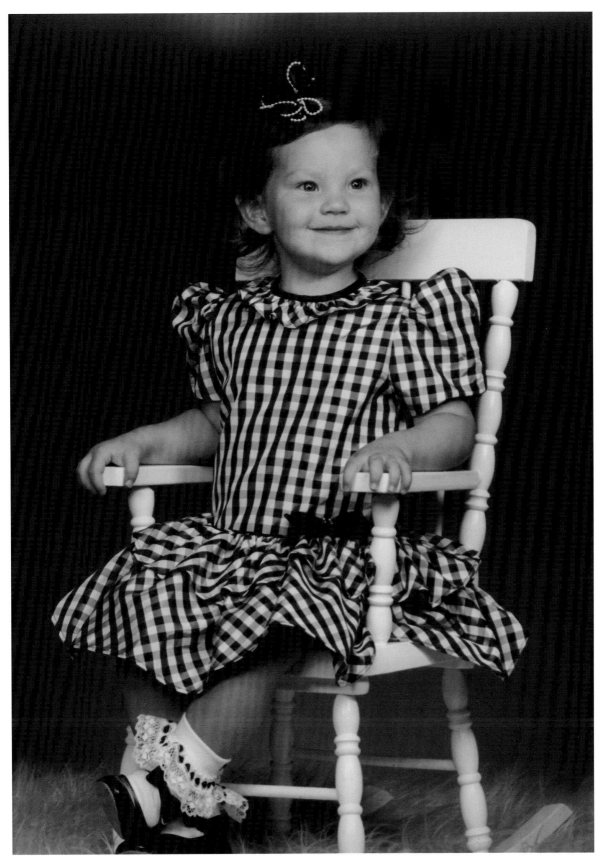

Francie Love, the first member of what Tom calls G3—the third generation.

COAST TO COAST

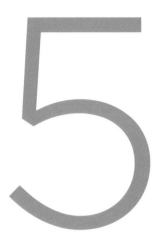

5

After thirty-three years of incremental growth, the Love's chain of Country Stores and Travel Stops was approaching critical mass in 1997. There were 120 stores with more than 2,000 employees scattered across the states of Oklahoma, Texas, Arkansas, Kansas, New Mexico, Colorado, and Arizona. With almost half of those stores concentrated in the state of Oklahoma, there was plenty of room for expansion within that territory and a world of possibilities beyond.

For Tom Love, there was no question about the next step in the evolution of his

Although the first to give credit to others who kept Love's competitive, profitable, and growing, Tom Love remained the face and spirit of the company as it entered the 21st Century.

family-owned enterprise. The company would grow. That determination was in part a reflection of his own personality, but just as important, it was an outgrowth of his confidence in the business plan he and his team had assembled and the obstacles they had overcome. When he told a reporter that "Love's is going to set the gold standard for people on the go," it was not so much a boast as it was a simple expression of his own conviction they were on the road to success.

Tom also knew that road was full of potholes, detours, and falling rocks. On all sides pushing back were his competitors, such as TA, Petro, Pilot, and Flying J, with deeper pockets of financial resources, more years of experience, and similar commitments to expansion. Ironically, an even more serious challenge would be dealing with the consequences of self-imposed success. How would they borrow the escalating amounts of money needed to buy land and build stores? How would they find the team leaders who could balance the simultaneous challenges of expansion and operational efficiencies? How would they maintain the entrepreneurial spirit to seek new opportunities as the company feasted on the bounty of proven success?

If they were going to transform their company from a promising regional enterprise to a major chain of travel stops stretching from coast to coast, Tom Love and his leadership team needed to gather all the pieces of the puzzle, assemble them into a focused image, and never let the players see the boundaries of what was possible.

They found a pivot point in 1997.

When Tom told a reporter that "Love's is going to set the gold standard for people on the go," it was not so much a boast as it was a simple expression of his own conviction they were on the road to success.

"The economy was fragile at the time," Doug Stussi remembers, "and capital was difficult to find, especially for a highly leveraged company like Love's. We were the small guy, trying to sneak up on Petro, Pilot, Flying J, and our other competitors."

The governor on growth was money for capital investment. In the 1960s, Tom had overcome that limitation by leasing abandoned filling stations. In the 1970s, he had turned to local bankers who wanted to see economic development in their hometowns. In the 1980s, he had found solutions such as lease-backs that used third-party investors to assume the initial capitalization and let positive cash flow pay off the debt over a number of years. By the late 1990s, with the cost of one Love's store on the interstate highway system rising to the range of $3 million to $5 million, he and his leadership team needed to find new sources for capital investment.

The traditional means of transforming a promising enterprise with potential into an investment grade business with bold ambitions was to go public through an initial stock offering and shared ownership with outside investors. Along with the stockpile of cash, however, came compromise and control from stock holders, board members, and analysts on Wall Street who demanded short term results measured by the quarter rather than long term gains measured by value. Tom Love, who admittedly did not like working within the structured system of a board, was never tempted to take that path.

Instead, he and his son Greg turned to their time tested combination of finding the right person, at the right time, who could take advantage of new opportunities. In 1997, the right time arrived with the growing consolidation of local and national banks into multi-level financial giants with the resources to invest huge sums of cash that would have overwhelmed even the biggest, most entrepreneurial state banks only a decade earlier. And fortunately for Tom and Greg, the right person came along at that critical moment. His name was Doug Stussi.

Born in Kansas City, Doug moved to Oklahoma City at a young age in 1963. His father, a natural salesman, ran a plant manufacturing automatic doors and his mother eventually got into sales. Doug went to the University of Oklahoma and majored in business administration with an emphasis in accounting. His first job after graduating in 1978 was with the national accounting firm of Arthur Andersen, where he audited a growing little company called Love's Country Stores. The chief financial officer of Love's offered him a job, but it did not pay enough to be tempting.

In 1980, with Oklahoma's economy soaring during the oil and gas boom in the Deep Anadarko Basin, Doug moved to Continental Federal Savings and Loan where he spent six years as chief financial officer and another six years as chief operating officer. At the time, Love's was one of Continental's key customers. Unfortunately for

Doug and his family, the bank succumbed to the region's second Great Depression and widespread bank failure. As Tom phrased the result, "Doug had to turn the lights out."

After four years at another company, Doug was talking to his neighbor, Terry Ross, a vice president at Love's who suggested he talk to Greg about a job. He interviewed and was hired as controller in charge of accounting, preparation of financial reports, and audits. In 1997, just as the company was gearing up for another burst of accelerated growth, Doug was named chief financial officer with responsibilities for finances, legal work, tax preparation, and most importantly, the management of banking relationships.

"When I assumed the duties as CFO in 1997, the company was doing well," Doug recalled almost twenty years later, "but Tom and Greg wanted more, and they needed a back office willing to charge up the next hill with them." That hill was steep and full of obstacles. "The economy was fragile at the time," Doug remembers, "and capital was difficult to find, especially for a highly leveraged company like Love's. We were the small guy, trying to sneak up on Petro, Pilot, Flying J, and our other competitors."

Paula Downing, the former CFO, left behind a solid base of local and regional banking support, especially Liberty National Bank, which had survived the banking crisis in Oklahoma after 1985, and Boatmens, which had taken over the assets of First National Bank of Oklahoma City. Other financing came from a couple of banks in Kansas City and a few insurance companies. As a long-time veteran among local bankers, Doug quickly reached out to that diversified list of what he called "capital partners," but knew he needed to cultivate relationships with bigger banks with greater resources.

To go upstream in the national banking system, Love's had to turn the corner from being seen as an entrepreneurial model with ambition to an investment grade business with a solid future. Doug also had to find a way around the fact that traditional debt-to-equity formulas did not reflect the true value of a company that regularly invested huge amounts in land and construction, which in turn affected short term profit margins. Like his predecessors, Doug had to convince bankers and insurance company executives in New York, San Francisco, and North Carolina that Love's positive cash flow and historically low operating costs made his company a good bet and worthy of lower interest rates.

The Love's management team accomplished that mission with transparency and communication. A key player in that undertaking was Shane Wharton, who came to Love's with Doug in 1996 and took over accounting duties the next year. Years later, Doug would

To go upstream in the national banking system, Love's had to turn the corner from being seen as an entrepreneurial model with ambition to an investment grade business with a solid future.

recall his contributions to turning the corner in 1997: "Shane, who had been a senior auditor with KPMG and controller for Data Times Corp, developed a new profit and loss statement that not only helped reassure our capital partners that we were on the right track, but also gave our operations team the tools to measure best practices and reward high achievers."

Doug, Shane, and their accounting team could show that Love's had never been on the ropes. "We clearly illustrated our long term ability to turn the dial up when possible and down when necessary," recalled Doug. "Either way, they could see that we were nimble enough that we were not going to lose money." In 1999, Doug initiated quarterly group meetings with capital partners, including both local account executives and national vice presidents. Once a year, they would meet at the Love's headquarters building in Oklahoma, twice a year by telephone conference, and once a year at a location where the bankers could tour a Love's Travel Stop. Doug wanted the bankers to see the quality of the people running the company.

The efforts paid off in the long term. When Tom and his top managers decided to diversify into both mid-stream fuel trading and transportation logistics, they not only had a line of credit for investment, but also enjoyed a level of trust among the bankers and insurance company managers that they could survive initial setbacks that might otherwise spook short term investors. When a prolonged price war with competitors put pressure on profit margins, the executives could see how Love's would absorb the impact. And when the Great Recession of 2008 shook the confidence of investors around the world, Love's capital partners did not panic. After a short lull while the initial smoke cleared, Tom, Greg, and their team resumed aggressive expansion plans and never worried about where the capital funds would come from.

At the end of the day, all of the transparency and good relationships with capital partners depended on one key factor–performance–which was measured in cold, hard numbers pulled from cash flow, operating costs, and net profit. While those numbers could fluctuate for a number of reasons, they were affected most by efficient operations. And by 1997, Tom recognized that something was not quite right with the operations.

Love's had grown, both in geographical area and number of stores, but the operational systems that had worked well in small town convenience stores was no longer a good fit for larger, more ambitious travel stops on the interstate highway system. He needed something better, but more importantly, he needed someone who

Love's had grown, but the operational systems that had worked well in small town convenience stores was no longer a good fit for larger, more ambitious travel stops on the interstate highway system. Tom needed someone who could analyze their operations and create a road map to the future. That person proved to be Tom Edwards.

could analyze their operations and create a road map to the future. That person proved to be Tom Edwards.

Edwards was born in a small community in Iowa, where his father farmed and operated a coal mine. He played college football for a year, then quit the team, got married, and finished his degree with a major in management and marketing and a minor in accounting. To pay his way through college, he worked the night shift at a service station where he pumped gas and studied between customers. His first job out of college was with Super America, a high performing and widely admired convenience store chain based in Minneapolis, Minnesota. For the next twelve years, he worked his way up through the company from store manager and district manager to marketing manager with sixty stores in five states. "Super America was recognized nationally for its efficient operations," remembered Edwards. "It was a great place to learn and grow."

In 1983, after one year working for a contract staffing firm, Edwards took a job as vice president of operations with a small but promising truck stop company called Pilot. "Like other start-up companies taking advantage of trucking deregulation and interstate highways, we were stumbling and bumbling, trying to figure out how to make our system work," Edwards recalled. "No one had a blue print for success, so we would launch a plan and see what worked." For twelve years, Edwards learned valuable lessons on the job and helped Pilot break out of its regional footprint.

When Edwards left Pilot in 1994, he signed a non-compete clause preventing him from working for another truck stop company for three years. He built his own Pilot store in Georgia, complete with a Steak n' Shake cafe and SUBWAY. Despite that success, he wanted to work for another expanding company, so in 1997 he sold his store to Pilot and sent resumes to several travel stop companies, including Love's. He had an offer from a company in Arizona, but before he accepted, he sent one more message to Tom Love, who quickly responded this time. After two interviews, he was offered a job as special projects coordinator with Love's. His first day on the job was May 11, 1997.

Years later, Edwards remembered those first two months at Love's. "Tom Love did not know exactly what he needed, but he knew he needed a bigger and better armed team if he was going to grow his company into a national chain," Edwards later recalled. "After forty-five days on the job, I was asked if I had an opinion of what was wrong and what I would do about it. I quickly wrote and presented a 25-step plan." In August of 1997, only three months after joining the Love's team, Edwards was named vice president of operations.

At a critical turning point in the company's history, Tom Edwards brought his hard edged demand for consistency and teamwork to Love's in 1997.

Edwards brought a new attitude and style of operations to Love's. By his own admission, he was extremely aggressive and quick to pull the trigger when it was time to make a decision. He would listen to other opinions, but once a decision was made and a standard was adopted, he expected everyone to be on the same page. "You can't let everybody do their own thing," he said. "As a group we are constantly looking for best practices, and if you find that, everyone has to do it that way." He also was competitive, which was a good match for Tom Love's approach to business. "Every day we get up, we have to feel like we've got to work harder, to be better than our competition," Edwards said. "I never think we are the best."

The travel stop veteran brought to Love's more than twenty years of experience. "I never pretended to be a frontier kind of guy," he recalled. "I didn't want to be the first guy out with anything...let somebody else try it and let's look at it for a while." One time, a person in the company said he was blessed with common sense. He responded that life-long experience, making mistakes and learning lessons over time, creates common sense. To gain even more experience and share his vision of best practices, Edwards quickly proved that he was willing to finish what he started. For years, he would be on the road, visiting store teams four out of five days a week. He later admitted, "I don't know how to slow down."

Tom Edwards (center) assembled an operations management team that included these former colleagues at Pilot. They are (from left to right) Bob Greufe, Mark Romig, Kym Van Dyke, former employee Dave Carter, Clint Bennison, Jim Xenos, Dion Crider, Rick Shuffield, former employee Alan Byrd, David Frankenfield, and Brent Bergevin.

Edwards quickly realized that a change in management style alone was not enough to achieve Tom Love's goals. The organization, he believed, needed a new philosophy at the top levels of operational management, starting at the stores. For decades, the goal of offering the cheapest gas in town had fostered a culture based on keeping operational costs at the bare minimum, which included asking all staff members to multi-task and accept a pay scale that was one of the lowest in the industry.

That approach had worked well enough for two reasons when the company was small and growing incrementally. One was the ability and time to develop managers from within. The other was Tom Love's ability to foster personal loyalty to himself. To break out of a cycle that either wore down managers or made them tempting targets for better-paying competitors, Love's needed a new approach to management if the company was going to grow.

It all came down to recruiting, developing, and retaining top managers. While developing talent was achieved through setting clear goals, communication, and training, recruitment and retention were tied to the hard reality of compensation. Good people, working hard and putting in long hours, had always been motivated as much by pay as by pride. While at Pilot, Tom Edwards had seen the benefits of vested profit sharing as a form of motivation. Within his first year at Love's, he suggested to Tom and Greg that they adopt a similar system. Their response was called Love's Shares.

In essence, Love's shares set aside a percentage of profits each year for distribution to managers from the store level to vice presidents. Not only was it a good recruiting tool, but it also was a tool for retention through the rule of vesting. To receive all of their bonuses, managers had to stay with Love's at least seven years. As Tom Edwards would later describe it, the vested profit sharing was "a golden handcuff...once a person started vesting, it was hard to walk away when they had a bad day, and everyone has a bad day once in a while." And it worked, both in terms of recruitment and profits. The first class in line to vest made more in bonuses in 1998 than the entire company had made in profits in 1997.

The new compensation package, combined with Tom Edwards' aggressive and demanding management style, had both an immediate and long lasting impact. Out of thirty district and divisional managers in the field in 1997, only three were still working for Love's in 1999, two of whom left initially but came back with the encouragement of Edwards. One of those who made the transition was Mike Herman, who would eventually serve the company as director of convenience stores. The other was Kevin Asbury, a long

"Every day we get up, we have to feel like we've got to work harder, to be better than our competition," Edwards said. "I never think we are the best."

time employee who had joined Love's as a manager in training in 1986. He would eventually serve as vice president of human services and vice president of operations.

In his first few years at Love's, Edwards recruited a generation of operational managers who would still be leading the company fifteen years later. Some had worked with him at Pilot, so he knew their potential and they knew his expectations. Included in those he cherry picked from the lower management ranks of Pilot were Brent Bergevin, who would eventually lead the Gemini trucking and terminal business; Rick Shuffield, who would rise to become Greg Love's field

For the Love family, unified vision and efficient operations were not enough for long term growth. If the company was to sustain the momentum started after 1997, they needed to focus on the core values that had helped them reach that pivot point. Years later, those core values would be summarized in this brochure.

lieutenant in charge of real estate development; Jim Xenos, who would become vice president of technology; Clint Bennison, who would become a key operations director; Kym Van Dyke, who would work with Rick in real estate; Mark Romig, who came a few years later but would become director of merchandising; and Bob Greufe, another who came a few years later and became the eventual division director for all travel stops west of Oklahoma City. Instead of waiting to work their way up the ranks at Pilot, each of them was attracted to the potential of quick upward mobility at Love's.

Although essential for further growth, the addition of Doug Stussi as chief financial officer and Tom Edwards as executive vice president of operations did not complete the circle of leadership Tom Love needed if his company was going to break out of its regional footprint in 1997. He needed reinforcements at the ownership level, and with his commitment to family ownership, that meant he needed to include his own children in the evolution of the company. He needed to close the family circle of leadership, not only for the present, but also for the future.

Tom understood the challenges of passing the baton of leadership from one generation to another. He had seen family-owned businesses where the founder tenaciously held on to all decisions, but tried to include his or her children with passive, supporting duties devoid of real importance. He had seen other family enterprises fail to make the generational transition when siblings fought each other

---

h reporters, participates in business reviews and iar with the concept of integrity on the job and

at does it mean to you?
pend. This is easy to say but not always as easy to es to live with integrity. And there are many folks hich everyone should be proud.

ing
a
rity
cuts

TY

does integrity help us get ahead
ns and especially about people. We pride ourselves parts of our company, from operations to the fleet hey can count on us when we make a commitment. mmunicate, transparency is important for our rela-

mbodies the spirit of integrity. Why
n reaching it. Whether it was fighting the British or rait in today's world.

Frank Love, President of Love's Operating Companies, is no stranger to innovative thinking. The Love's Family of Companies have seen tremendous growth in recent years made possible in large part by following through on ideas that seemed beyond the norm at the time. It took innovative thinking and swift action from employees at every level to result in the success we see today.

What does creating new opportunities through innovative thinking mean to you?
When I look around at Love's, I see how innovative thinking has given us the opportunity to win new customers and be more effective than our competitors. We've had some pretty significant innovations in the past few years, including our model for the tire care business and the development of our oil logistics business. But the little innovations are what our customers notice. For example: when Dan Phillips was managing Joplin, Mo., and started using long-handled squeegees on the gasoline island to better serve big pickup trucks and mobile homes, he was using innovative thinking that made a difference for our customers. We now have long-handled squeegees available on our gas islands across the country. That's innovation anyone can do if you are focused on taking care of our customers.

Why is innovation an important core value in all areas and levels of the organization?
Innovative thinking creates opportunities that better serve our customers and help us be more competitive. From the corporate office team member who finds a new way to be more productive in their job to a store cashier who figures out a better way to satisfy our customers, innovative thinking is what sets us apart from the competition – normally through better service or cost savings. One more thing: those at Love's who display this type of effort are typically more successful in their jobs and careers.

How have Love's, Gemini and Musket been able to grow through innovation?
The tire care business and oil logistics business that I mentioned earlier are significant growth examples in recent years. In both cases, we drew upon some of our core strengths in operations, efficiency and cost management to quickly become industry leaders. We recognized what we could do better than others, and we attacked the opportunity.

new **opportunities** **INNOVATIVE** thinking creating

What is ahead for the Love's Family of Companies?
Well, our truck stop growth plan over the next five years is significant. We will continue to capture trucking industry market share and build our brand into one of the most recognizable and appealing to highway travelers. Gemini and Musket will also continue to pursue an aggressive growth agenda and build upon previous successes.

What is the best leadership advice you've been given?
Do what you say you are going to do.

What is the best piece of advice you would give someone who aspires to be a leader at Love's?
Do what you say you are going to do, and out-hustle your competition.

As President of Love's Development Companies, Greg Love and his team certainly need to persevere as they grow the Love's Travel Stops network of locations through real estate purchases. He shared his thoughts about working through the daily challenges we all face.

What does perseverance mean to you?
As we have all experienced, life can be very difficult. When you encounter a challenging situation, instead of giving up, you forge ahead. Perseverance is just that -dealing with all of the difficulties of a challenging situation, but not giving up.

giving dealing challenging situation difficulties **PERSEVERANCE**

Why is perseverance an important core value at your level – and for all levels of employees?
The old saying, "If it was easy, everyone would be doing it," is very true. What everyone at Love's does throughout our day is not easy, from the consistent friendly customer service delivered by a fuel desk team member, to the safe delivery of fuel by a Gemini driver, or the help desk employee who supports the store manager. Consistently performing these jobs every day, sometimes under tough circumstances, is another way you could define perseverance.

How have you been able to grow the Love's footprint through perseverance?
Sometimes perseverance is being flexible, trying to learn what we can do differently to get where we need to. For example, there have been times when a store layout wasn't accepted by the City or State Department of Transportation. Rather than throwing in the towel, my team would work with the city to learn what modifications we might be able to make to satisfy their concerns. We may have to completely change how the traffic flows, or enters and exists. If the changes still allow us to properly take care of our customers, then we will make those modifications.

What is ahead for Love's in your area?
We continue to find and build 20-25 new Love's Travel Stops per year. Some will be larger than our average store, some smaller. We study the site and build what we feel is an appropriate size (amount of truck parking, truck fueling, square footage of building) for the individual site. The design of our buildings is a never-ending study, and it changes every year. In addition to our travel stop buildings continually evolving, the tire shop buildings continue to grow and change. We will continue to aggressively grow this business with tire shops at all new stores and add new tire shops to our existing network of stores.

What is the best piece of leadership advice you've been given in your career?
Know what you are doing. People won't follow someone who doesn't have credibility. If those you are trying to lead don't respect your job knowledge or ability, you won't be successful as a leader.

What is the best piece of advice you'd give an employee who aspires to be a leader at a Love's company?
There is no substitute for hard work. Know your stuff. Treat your co-workers with respect. Learn what you enjoy doing. You will always be more effective doing a job that you look forward to.

---

over direction and control, and without unified vision, few companies survived. Tom thought the Love family could avoid both pitfalls.

He and Judy knew their children and recognized the assets they could bring to the company. Each had a distinctive personality, but they shared a bond of love and trust Tom thought could survive the pressures of the business world. Just as important, his own leadership style was based on collaboration and trust. Just as he had delegated real authority to Larry Dillard, Lindell Pearson, Doug Stussi, and Tom Edwards, he was prepared to bring his children into the company with more than just a job and title. If they wanted to pursue a career in business, they would earn a place at the table and he would give them the authority to lead the company and the latitude to make mistakes. Hopefully, that spirit of trust and collegiality would pass down to future generations of the family.

Tom's faith in that plan was reinforced by the performance of Greg, the oldest son, who had already carved out a niche for himself in the leadership circle. He had started at the bottom, running a car wash and learning from both his father and company veterans, especially Lindell Pearson. By 1985, he was selecting sites for new stores, and by 1995 he was named president of the company. Tom, as chief executive officer and chairman of the board, increasingly relied on Greg to be his agent of growth as well as a voice of reason to temper his own enthusiasm for the next deal.

After college, Laura (second from right) decided to focus her energies on her three daughters, Liza, Caroline, and Claire.

Laura, the second born, did not want an active role in company management. Although she had majored in business at the University of San Diego, she decided her path in life was as a mother. By 1997, when her father was reconstituting his leadership team, she was busy with her three children and an active life. Like Judy, who had given up her accounting duties at Love's by 1975, Laura would be part of leadership one step outside of the day-to-day circle of management.

Jenny, like Greg, had already earned a place at the management table. She started in food service, where she was part of the development team that experimented with quick service restaurants, and created the office of corporate communications. She continued the in-house newsletter, *Love's Country*, as a means to preserve a sense of family among all employees as the company grew both in numbers and distance apart. She also became the spokesperson for Love's, responding to reporters' questions and working with district and store managers to generate publicity for openings. After the turn of the century, Jenny would assume more responsibility for team building, branding, and philanthropy, often spending the majority of her week traveling with the operations team and building strong relationships with the teams in the field. Her brothers often point out that the first question team members ask them when they walk into a store is, "How is your dad?" The second question is, "Where is Jenny?"

Tom's and Judy's fourth child was Frank Criner Love, named in honor of Tom's father, F.C., who had risen to the president's office of Kerr-McGee Energy Corporation. As a youth, the younger Frank worked at a Love's store and mowed lawns during the summer. He excelled at football, played at the University of San Diego, and later transferred to the University of Oklahoma, where he completed a degree in English.

After graduation, Frank moved to Colorado and took a job as a waiter at the newly opened Ritz-Carlton Hotel, known for its high standards, consistency, and customer service. By his second year with the hotel, he was a kitchen manager, which meant he and his team were responsible for all the dishes, from dishwashing and inventory to making sure banquets had the proper flatware and silverware.

After college and a few years in the hotel industry, Frank joined the Love's team in 1994.

In August of 1994, Frank moved back to Oklahoma when he became engaged to his future wife, who was attending the University of Oklahoma. He worked briefly at the experimental Love's restaurant in Erick called Cowboys, became assistant manager at a Love's south of Oklahoma City on I-35, and moved in 1995 to Weatherford, Texas, to open and operate a new Travel Stop. In 1997, now married, Frank became part of a special projects team that soon included a new hire named Tom Edwards. For the next six months, Frank worked with Tom as they analyzed operations and developed what Tom Edwards called his 25 steps to higher performance at Love's. One clear opportunity was to market vast amounts of diesel fuel to truck fleets. Love's was on the verge of being big enough to tap that market, and Frank was uniquely suited to build a team to tackle it.

Frank Love, closing the family circle of leadership, was tasked with this new marketing effort. Little did his father know what that decision would do for the company.

Since 1981, the overwhelming bulk of customers buying diesel fuel at Love's Travel Stops had been independent owner-operators who did not drive enough miles to get discounts from the big national truck stop companies. Their only way to cut costs was to buy the cheapest fuel in town, which usually was found at a Love's. As competition for the owner-operator sector grew more intense in the late 1990s, the Love's management team launched an incentive program called "I Love Rewards." For every dollar spent on diesel fuel, a truck driver received a one penny credit that could be used to buy food or merchandise at a Love's. Within a decade, more than 250,000 truck drivers carried an "I Love Rewards" card.

Although the incentive program and low prices maintained market share among owner-operators, it did little to attract the increasing volume of truck drivers working for the big regional and national transport companies that had grown phenomenally through consolidation of smaller start-ups. At those big companies, the decision for buying fuel was made not by the drivers, but by owners or purchasing agents who used their volume of business to negotiate discounts from travel stop operators spanning their territory.

Among the modern giants were J.B. Hunt, founded by Johnnie Bryan Hunt in Northwest Arkansas. From five trucks and seven trailers in 1961, the company grew to 550 trucks three years after deregulation and would expand to 12,000 trucks by 2012. Schneider National, founded in 1938 in Wisconsin, would grow to 14,000 trucks and 18,000 drivers. The biggest of the new trucking breed would be Swift Transportation, founded in Los Angeles in 1966. It would explode from 800 trucks in 1990 to 16,000 trucks in 2012. By the late 1990s, this potential new market was too big to ignore.

Within months, Love's had a team in the field knocking on doors trying to make deals with owners and purchasing agents. Frank, who assembled the crew, spent the better part of two years calling on ten to fifteen trucking companies a week. Although not always successful, he was learning what potential customers wanted and building relationships that would pay off later. The biggest obstacle to early success was the regional footprint of Love's, which did not appeal to the big trucking companies driving coast to coast.

Some of Frank's early team members would stay around as that changed. Danny Peyton, the first person hired, would later work for a competitor, but come back to Love's. Chris Dexter, who would eventually rise to become Love's national account manager, was hired after he sold Frank a trade show booth. "It was the best sales job and the worst trade show booth I had ever seen," Frank recalled later, "so I hired him a week later." Another early team member knocking on the doors of the big truck companies was Jon Archard, who would later become the director of sales.

While fleet sales were slow at first, those early efforts would eventually pay big dividends as the Love's network spread across the

"We made it a point of pride to always be very straight with every customer," Frank remembers, "and we would tell them what we could and could not do...if we could not satisfy their needs at the present time, we told them we would be back when we could."

country. It started with hard work and tenacity, building relationships by showing up every month whether the customer was doing a lot or no business at all with Love's. The team also built a reputation for integrity. "We made it a point of pride to always be very straight with every customer," Frank remembers, "and we would tell them what we could and could not do...if we could not satisfy their needs at the present time, we told them we would be back when we could."

Fleet accounts, while increasing the volume of diesel sold, squeezed the margin of profit on every gallon passing through the pumps at a time when competition was becoming more intense, especially in states where Love's was going head to head with Flying J and Pilot, the main two competitors with similar low price strategies. From 2002 to 2008, Flying J was especially aggressive, and when Love's would not back down, a prolonged price war kept profit margins on diesel at the bare minimum.

In the travel stop industry, there were three ways to make a profit: one from the top, one to the side, and one on the bottom. On top was the price of the product sold, which was capped by competition and demand, both of which were difficult to control. To the side was volume, which could be partially controlled through increased market share, such as fleet sales and additional stores, which took time to build. On the bottom was the cost to deliver that

The corporate name of Musket was recycled for a new logistical arm of the company. Among the growing assets of the venture was this fuel terminal in Kingman, Arizona.

Although Oklahoma Tank Lines would continue to deliver fuel to Love's stores in Oklahoma and surrounding states, the logistical needs of keeping all stores wet with fuel from coast to coast was given to the in-house enterprise called Gemini (above and below).

product, which included both operational expenses and the whole-sale price of the product itself.

While Tom Edwards and his team were working hard every day to keep quality high and net operating expenses low, the teams led by Greg and Frank Love were expanding the number of stores and landing fleet accounts to increase the volume of sales and market share. The only other strategy available to them was to lower the cost of getting the product to the pump, which required a combination of aggressive fuel trading and logistical support to get the fuel to the right place, at the right time, as cheaply as possible. For the next decade, the Love's team would expand their capabilities to do both. One venture was called Gemini; the other was a reinvented Musket.

Aggressive fuel purchasing had always been a fundamental component of the Love's business plan. Tom Love, working under the corporate name of Musket in 1964, was the original purchasing agent, striking deals with refiners and relying on low rack prices while avoiding long term contracts in his quest to have the cheapest gas in town. When the Arab Oil Embargo limited supply, Tom and Terry Ross redoubled their efforts to keep their Country Stores wet and expanded the network of refineries where they bought fuel.

As their network grew, the name of Musket was pushed to the side and the company was re-incorporated as Love's Travel Stops & Country Stores.

In 2000, while Tom and Greg pushed Love's territory in all directions with new stores, Frank pulled the name Musket back to the forefront and began hiring talented industry veterans to build it into a fuel trading arm of the company. The first man on the team was Mike Brakefield, a native of Oklahoma who had graduated from the University of Oklahoma and worked for Exxon-Mobil, where he rose through the ranks to become a terminal manager working with supply and distribution. When he brought that experience to Love's, he was given the task to focus on growth and seize new opportunities while making sure they could always offer the lowest cost fuel at every store every day.

Musket's team of fuel traders scoured the market to find the lowest prices, and they had to do it throughout the day in each market where they had a Love's to supply. Usually, the best prices were found at refineries, but the cost of shipping had to be calculated into the cost. Sometimes, they would buy at a terminal, where the cost of transport by pipeline was already added. Other times, they might buy at a refinery and ship it themselves. In the post-Arab Oil Embargo world market, the price could change several times a day, so the purchasing agents had to consider not only the price at any given moment, but also the demand and storage capacity at each store and the timing and costs of shipping. It was like a three-dimensional jigsaw puzzle, converting information into action.

In 2002, heeding their directive to look for opportunities, the Musket team found a new way to supply stores with the cheapest fuel and open the door to a new enterprise at the same time. It was called fuel-by-rail. Shell Oil, which operated several refineries along the Gulf Coast, had discovered they could ship refined diesel to the booming states of Arizona and Nevada by rail and still make money after calculating the costs of transport. They offered to supply Musket with fuel if Love's would build terminals and a rail fleet, a concept that Mike Brakefield had seen in New England during his days with Mobil. They did and both companies made money.

The Musket team led by Frank took the concept to a higher level and created an integrated fuel trading and supply enterprise. They started in 2005 with a wholesale fuel-distribution company with offices in Phoenix, Arizona, followed by additional offices in Houston, Texas, and Calgary, Canada, supplying both Love's and third-party customers in the region where they had a price advantage. They also leased diesel tanks on the Gulf Coast so they could buy directly from refiners. Ultimately, Musket would control more than two million barrels of storage capacity.

The Love's leadership team followed those bold steps with the

As Musket fuel trading grew after 2001, the logistical advantages gained helped Love's survive a decade of intense price wars and emerge with a national footprint that still offered "the cheapest fuel in town."

decision to lease their own rail cars, buy the fuel wherever they could get the best price, and ship it themselves throughout the Southwest where Love's had stores. The only limitation was the distance from the terminal to the stores, and because the volume needed in many rural areas did not justify the cost of new terminals, they needed a way to get the fuel from the rail cars to the travel stops in the most efficient way. Again, the Musket team created an opportunity. It was called a trans-loader.

Love's received a patent for a portable trans-load trailer that could be pulled up to a rail car on a siding and pump the fuel to a truck on the other side. At its most efficient level, a unit train of 104 leased rail cars would be loaded with fuel bought at the best price at a refinery, pulled to eastern Arizona under contract with the Burlington Northern/Santa Fe Railroad Company, and scattered to a number of sites where trans-loaders pumped the fuel into trucks for distribution to Love's Travel Stops and other customers. By eliminating both the wholesale and distribution middle men, Musket saved money, made additional profits, and improved flexibility of supply. By 2007, the successful operation grew to 2,500 leased rail cars, thirty trans-load units, and four terminals across the western United States. Then disaster struck.

The worst economic crisis since the 1930s, called the Great Recession of 2008, shook the world economy to its knees. In the American Southwest, especially in Arizona and Nevada where the housing bubble had inflated the most, the economy screeched to a virtual standstill. Overnight, the demand for fuel dropped dramatically and with it went the price advantage of shipping fuel over long distances. Musket, after investing a small fortune in fuel-by-rail infrastructure and manpower, had the means to move vast volumes of fuel over long distances but no customers to serve. Once again, they needed a new opportunity and a new person to lead the attack.

The new team leader was J.P. Fjeld-Hansen, a native of Norway who had spent two years in officer's training in the Norwegian Navy before coming to the United States and attending the University of Texas. He began his career in the oil business working on rigs off the Gulf Coast and off-shore Alaska. He joined Musket in February of 2007 and became director of trading in May of 2008. He was just getting settled in when the Musket team found their way out of a crisis. It was in North Dakota.

Since the 1950s, geologists had known that the Bakken formation in the Williston Basin held vast stores of oil locked in dense shale. The only problem was the lack of technology to extract it. In 2008, that challenge was overcome through a combination of

Love's received a patent for a portable trans-load trailer that could be pulled up to a rail car on a siding and pump the fuel to a truck on the other side.

horizontal drilling and high pressure fracturing. With estimates of recoverable oil ranging from seven to twenty-four billion barrels in a 200,000 square mile area of North Dakota, Montana, and southern Canada, the boom was on. Then the oil companies found they did not have the infrastructure, especially pipelines, to move the oil to distant refineries and markets.

The Musket team filled that void with an innovative solution. They transferred their trans-loaders and leased rail cars to North Dakota, where they were converted to pump and carry the light sweet crude from the Bakken to tank farms in Cushing, Oklahoma, and refineries on the Gulf Coast. As one of the first to tap the market, they secured enough contracts to justify building a full unit-train terminal where 104-car trains could be loaded with 70,000 barrels of oil in one twenty-four-hour shift. In one nimble move, a new, profitable business rose from the ashes of what had looked like a total loss.

Other than direct profit, the fleet of rail cars capable of carrying either crude oil or refined fuel gave Musket and Love's improved flexibility to cope with challenges and take advantage of opportunities. After the devastation of Hurricane Ike, rail cars were diverted to the American Southeast loaded with fuel to keep Love's stores wet.

As Musket expanded into fuel by rail, Frank and his team purchased several shuttle wagons to assemble and redirect rail cars at their terminals.

In another case, a major pipeline company entered bankruptcy in the desert Southwest, which disrupted the flow and spiked the cost of fuel. Again, Musket rail cars were diverted to Houston, where fuels were blended and shipped to Love's stores within forty-eight hours. For a company rapidly growing coast to coast under the pressure of intense competition, that flexibility to move huge quantities of fuel quickly over vast distances was a critical advantage. From 2008 to 2013, Musket would maintain rail terminals in North Dakota, Wyoming, Colorado, Utah, Oklahoma, Texas, and Canada.

A similar advantage, although on a different scale, had developed alongside the fuel trading and fuel-by-rail initiatives since 2000. It was called Gemini Transport, named in honor of the birth of twin babies to Frank and his wife the same year. As they were doing with the fleet salesmen and fuel traders at Musket, Tom and Frank Love wanted Gemini to foster growth and seize new opportunities at a time when the chain of Love's stores was outgrowing the Oklahoma-based carrier of choice, Oklahoma Tank Lines, and was approaching the scale of operations that could support an in-house trucking enterprise. And once again, the right person rose to the occasion at the right time. His name was Brent Bergevin.

Brent grew up in Wisconsin, where his father worked more than four decades for the Chicago Northwest Railroad. At the age of

In 2005, as the gradual transition from Oklahoma Tank Lines to Gemini was gaining momentum, the value of this last leg in the logistics chain was proven at a time of crisis...Hurricane Katrina,

Transporting fuel to isolated locations within the Love's trade territory grew in complexity as the number of stores exceeded 200 on the way to 300. Oklahoma Tank LInes (right), had been a partner since the 1970s, but increasingly, the in-house Gemini truck fleet (facing page) was needed for a network that stretched from coast to coast.

fourteen, Brent started working part time in a full-service gasoline
station and worked his way up to become manager of the station
across the street from Lambeau Field in Green Bay. After completing college at the University of Wisconsin-Milwaukee, he took a job
with Shell Oil in Houston, where he worked his way up to district
manager of service stations. He left Shell, managed a small group of
truck stops scattered from Tulsa to Corpus Christi, and was recruited to Pilot. He started running truck stops under the watchful eye
of Tom Edwards in the summer of 1992.

In 1997, Brent was one of the middle managers who came to
Love's with Tom. He started in operations, eventually rising to division
manager over all travel stops west of Oklahoma City, but five years later,
recognizing the need to grow the truck initiative, he was tapped to
lead Gemini. In 2002, with six trucks and a handful of company drivers, Brent started building a team. He remembers Frank telling him,
"Grow as fast as possible with safety as your number one priority."

The first trucks, bought from a Freightliner dealer in Oklahoma
City, pulled trailer tanks illustrated with the photograph of Will Rogers, the Cherokee humorist, writer, and actor born near Claremore,
Oklahoma. In 2003, Tom Love had a better idea when he saw a truck
on the road hauling fuel for a convenience store chain. Its trailer
was painted a bright red. Tom suggested painting Love's trailers with

the same yellow used on the stores. Although Brent remembers his doubts about the plan, he had them painted with the company colors, name, and signature echo hearts. The design won an award from the American Trucking Association for best looking truck.

The drivers were expected to be just as sharp. Brent understood that the trucks were mobile billboards, representing Love's on the road and in the stores. He wanted the drivers to look good, proudly wear their name badges, and act like the professionals they were. He found that he did not need to recruit new drivers; they came to him based on word of mouth and personal references. When asked if he hired at certain times of the year, he said no, he was always in a hiring mode. Within a few years, he kept a marker board in his office with a color-coded list of openings, names of those hired but not yet on board, and names of those in training. All new hires went through a thorough background check and safety training.

In 2005, as the gradual transition from Oklahoma Tank Lines to Gemini was gaining momentum, the value of this last leg in the logistics chain was proven at a time of crisis. Hurricane Katrina, one of the deadliest natural disasters in American history, cut a

"We are the Southwest Airlines of fuel hauling," said Brent Bergevin in one interview.

When Tom suggested a new paint scheme for the Gemini truck fleet, Brent Bergevin expressed doubt. When the plan was implemented, the design won a national award.

wide swath through the Gulf Coast states and left in its wake death and destruction on an unprecedented scale. With normal means of fuel distribution disrupted, the Love's leadership team turned to Gemini to transfer fuel from all parts of the country to the affected region. Tom Love responded by telling Brent to "go all in." Not one store ran out of gas during the crisis.

The logistics management system, which had become more sophisticated over the years, was transferred to the Gemini team in Oklahoma City. Each dispatcher had access to a deep well of information, from projections of how much fuel a store might use within a twelve-hour period to the ten lowest prices of fuel within a store's supply region. They had to know where drivers were located at any given time of the day, how much capacity they had, and where they could load the right amount of fuel at the lowest price in the quickest amount of time. It was a logistical jigsaw puzzle.

As the volume of fuel increased year after year, Brent's team constantly searched for efficiencies that would shave even the slightest cost of hauling it. To minimize loading time, they installed dual hose trees at stations so one truck could pump off either side at the same time. To reduce the weight of the truck, which allowed them to haul more fuel under the weight limits of each state, they replaced dual tires with what was called "super singles," which transferred 600 pounds of weight from the truck to the fuel. An even more incremental transfer of weight from truck to fuel was the conversion of truck tanks from four compartments to three, which removed one metal separation plate and its weight. "We are the Southwest Airlines of fuel hauling," said Brent Bergevin in one interview.

The logistical impact of Gemini was reflected in the number of rigs on the road. From 2008, when there were 165 Love's trucks hauling fuel, the numbers increased to 190 in 2010 and 235 in 2011. The number of drivers increased in tandem. By 2012, Gemini employed 547 drivers with expectations that the number would grow to 623 drivers in 2013. During an interview more than a decade after they started Gemini, Brent remembered what Frank told him: "Run it like your own company, in a safe way, with value for Love's." Brent added, "I took it personal."

With a motivated management team, logistical advantages, and a unified vision coming from family owners, Love's was ready to go coast to coast.

Since 1964, growth had been the one constant in the history of Love's, but after what Tom called "splitting the atom," the pace of growth exploded from coast to coast. New designs customized for local markets (right and bottom), the sense of family from the owners to front line team members (below to the right), and a willingness to take chances gave Love's a national footprint that filled the national map (facing page).

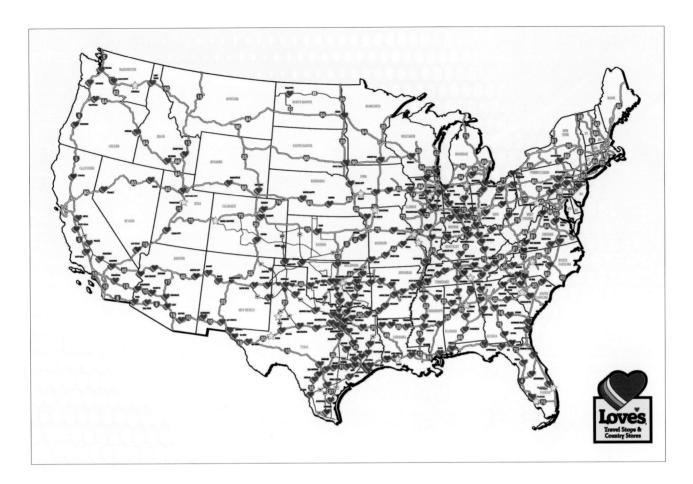

The transformation of Love's from a regional company to a national brand would be steady and organic rather than meteoric and flashy. In part, that ability to reduce risk and control growth was made possible by family ownership. "We flew under the radar of many people because we have always been committed to the long view," Greg Love recalled in an interview. Love's, according to Greg, did not need to impress existing or potential stockholders with dramatic announcements and boastful dreams. "As a private company," he added, "we could give an idea time to evolve."

With an aggressive management group and motivated employees, there was no shortage of ideas for confronting challenges and seizing opportunities. The task was sorting the good from the bad, which often took time and teamwork. The variables to be considered in each case often seemed endless and there was no playbook to consult. Facing a constantly changing marketplace and fierce competition, it was either change and grow or delay and shrink.

In 1997, when the Love's team planned only three new travel stops, the average size of a store was 5,000 square feet with five acres of land and six diesel bays located to one side so four-wheel drivers had access to gasoline pumps and parking places in front. The average cost for land and construction was $2.6 million. The layout of both the lot and the store had not changed much in

With a motivated management team, logistical advantages, and a unified vision coming from family owners, Love's was ready to go coast to coast.

seventeen years. Car customers walked in the front door, truckers came in a side door, and the bathrooms and walk-in coolers were in the back of the store to pull customers to and through the merchandise. Typically, the food service was located in the middle of the store flanked by separate check-out counters for car passengers and truckers.

The first subtle changes to this standard layout were prompted by increased truck traffic. After the initial burst of new start-up trucking companies following deregulation in 1980, there was a steady trend of consolidation into bigger transport companies that offered more efficiencies that ultimately increased long-distance freight hauled by trucks. Then came passage of the North American Free Trade Agreement in 1995, which added to the amount of freight hauled through Love's traditional territory in the Southwest. The challenge for the Love's management team was how to grab more of that growing market without losing their share of people traveling by automobile.

Adding to the challenge was the ever evolving world of quick service restaurants. In 1993, the Love's team had built its first branded restaurant inside a store. It was a Taco Bell Express that conveniently fit the space previously allocated to the Love's Fresh Daily Deli operation and offered a well known brand to pull travelers off the interstate. That was just the beginning. Over the next twenty years, Love's was in a race with competitors to get the right combination of food and brands in each store.

A turning point in that race was becoming a corporate franchisee for SUBWAY, which offered food that worked well in twenty-four-hour-a-day stores and advertised heavily across the country. By 2007, there were SUBWAYs in eighty-four Love's. Another turning point, after experimenting with brands such as Wendy's, Burger King, and Chester's Fried Chicken, was adding McDonald's to the system for the first time in 2005. The combination of a SUBWAY and a McDonald's in one store proved to be the best combination of food and branding to draw additional customers off the interstate. And for every customer stopping for food, Love's would normally sell another tank full of fuel and a few items of merchandise.

Merchandise was yet another factor affecting the size, layout, and cost of a store. While fuel had always been the primary profit center for Love's, merchandise added to a Country Store more than doubled the amount of fuel sold at any one stand-alone service station and generated another stream of profit at the same time. When truck drivers were added to the customer base, gear and tools were blended into the mix. By 1998 and the big expan-

The variety of restaurant food incorporated into Love's stores reflects a willingness to experiment with new combinations and adjust to regional variations across the country.

sion plans, each travel stop had what Greg Love would later describe as "an Ace Hardware store for truckers."

A growing line of gift items put pressure on the size of stores. By 2010, a typical Love's Travel Stop would carry a diverse mix of apparel, toys, and electronics. "Prices are competitive and the selection is impressive," wrote a reporter with a newspaper in Pauls Valley, Oklahoma. "Think televisions up to 22 inches, e-book readers, GPS and radar detectors, Rock Star Mickey, Mattel Barbie dolls, Hot Wheels, giant stuffed animals, and remote control helicopters. There are NASCAR and Oklahoma City Thunder jackets and hats, collectibles, and bling accessories such as purses, hats, and sandals for ladies."

In 2007, the volume and importance of merchandise was reflected in the creation of a new staff position at every store called assistant manager. They were supported by a central marketing staff at headquarters that would grow to sixteen people by 2012, when even a catch-all accounting column of "other income" alone had fifty-two categories that ranged from propane and video games to lottery tickets and ATM fees. Each new item placed a new demand on space and placement.

The first major changes in the size and layout of a Love's Travel Stop were apparent in nine new stores opened in 1999. At the suggestion of Tom Edwards, Greg Love and his team moved the restaurant from the middle of the building to one end of the store, with bathrooms for customers and showers for truckers at the other end. The change accomplished several goals. It created room to have an external door to the restaurant, which increased the visual appeal of any given brand, whether it was an Arby's or a SUBWAY. At the same time, the congestion in the middle of the store was eliminated, which encouraged more foot traffic to both packaged food and merchandise. The placement of check-out counters next to each other inside the front of the store created more flexible use of employees to keep lines from growing too deep and causing delays.

Other changes were made outside the store. As truck traffic increased, two more diesel bays were added, and where possible, separate curb-cut entries and exits were added for truck traffic, which in turn solved several problems. Curb appeal influenced families more than truck drivers, so moving the truck entries to side streets removed both congestion and the intimidation factor of dodging massive trucks and trailers. And moving the entry to the side of lots increased the room for turning big rigs and waiting in line for a bay to open.

From 1999 to 2012, as a result of all these changes, the cost of a typical Love's Travel Stop increased from $3.4 million to $9 million, while the size of typical stores grew from 5,000 to 10,000 square

The ability to manage inventory and sales results through innovative technology allowed Love's to expand and adjust merchandise by location and season.

feet and the average lot needed for a store doubled from five to ten acres, which created space for up to 80 cars and 100 trucks and recreational vehicles. Because the changes were incremental and custom designed for each location and market, few customers noticed the make-over while it was happening.

The team executing this evolution grew under the watchful eye of Greg Love, who as co-president with his brother Frank was responsible for Love's retail growth plan. Greg, who pulled the final

trigger on all new locations, increasingly relied on the vice president for construction and environment, his longtime colleague Terry Ross, and the director of real estate and development, Rick Shuffield.

Rick had started his career at Wendy's, where he rose to the position of area director. He moved to Pilot, working with Tom Edwards as a regional manager of operations, and came to Love's in the pivotal year of 1997. At first he joined Edwards as director of operations, but moved to real estate as Greg's duties on the leadership team broadened. With four project managers, Rick was responsible for finding new sites, getting them approved and permitted, and turning the site and plans over to the construction group.

Selecting a good location had always been more instinct than science, and it was becoming more difficult as the travel stop industry matured in the first decade of the new century and competitors raced each other to secure the best land along interstate highways. In the company newsletter, Greg explained the challenge. "We see fewer and fewer sites," he said, "that are located in areas where there is sufficient traffic, plenty of land, and a welcoming community eager for increased tax revenue and employment." A counterbalance to that limitation was Greg's experience in selecting good sites since 1985.

Typically, the real estate team tried to space Love's stores every 100 to 200 miles apart along an interstate highway or good four-lane diagonal with heavy truck traffic. They looked at traffic count, proximity to urban areas, visibility from the highway, and competition. After finding a potential site, the next task was getting permits, which could be straightforward and quick or complicated and time consuming. Issues that might arise included restrictive zoning, access to utilities, highway easements, storm water runoff, and nearby property owners. A common topic of negotiation was a Love's sign that rose 175 feet above the ground. Greg usually allowed for nine months to complete the permitting, but could remember a few cases where it took five years.

The construction phase usually took another six months, depending on weather. In 2010, Terry Ross described in the company newsletter what he called "a well oiled machine." They kept a pool of general contractors in each region of the country, but usually used a local contractor to install the fuel tanks. There were three companies that made canopies and two companies that built and installed signage. Instead of having the general contractor order specialty equipment, they handled it through the central office for reasons of consistency. Other direct purchases, either for consistency or savings, included structural steel, interior and exterior light-

...for every customer stopping for food, Love's would normally sell another tank full of fuel and a few items of merchandise.

ing, plumbing fixtures, and heat and air conditioning systems.

Each site could pose unique challenges. Most common in rural areas were the construction of water wells and waste system lagoons. At one site in Tupelo, Mississippi, crews had to replace all the dirt on a ten-acre lot because the "old dirt" would not support the foundations for the building or pump bays. At another site controlled by the Bureau of Land Management, Terry and his team had to post a qualified biologist on the construction site to watch for an endangered species of turtles.

There were exceptions to this pattern of site selection. In 2011, for example, the Love's leadership team decided to build three Love's Travel Stops in and around San Antonio, Texas. Although not separated by the standard distances preferred, each site had its own advantages that trumped the usual template. One was on the east side of San Antonio, near Seguin, at an intersection where truckers liked to fuel. All of Love's competitors were already there, so it was a hole in the network that needed to be filled for fleet sales. North of San Antonio, near Comfort, was a site with great visibility from the highway on a turnoff to the popular tourist destination of Fredericksburg. To the south of the city was a site surrounded by oil drilling activity which also strengthened Love's presence on I-35. All three stores, opened the same year, became successful operations.

As the size and shape of Love's Travel Stops evolved with each new location, the pace of new stores increased steadily from 1998 to 2012 with only a few temporary exceptions. From three stores opened in 1998, the pace hit nine stores in 1999, ten stores in 2000, and nine stores in 2001. After a slow year in 2002 when the number of new openings reached only six, the pace from 2003 to 2008 resumed with thirteen, twelve, ten, sixteen, fourteen, and fourteen stores. In 2009, in the shadow of the Great Recession, the number of new stores faded only slightly to nine. Then came an unprecedented leap forward in 2010.

Following the bankruptcy of Flying J in 2008, the Federal Trade Commission ruled that a proposed merger with Pilot would critically reduce competition in key areas of the interstate highway system where the trucking industry might have to pay more for fuel. As a result, twenty-six truck stops, some from the old Flying J system and some from the Pilot system, were sold to Love's. In that one transaction, Love's also gained a presence in the four states of New York, New Jersey, South Dakota, and Washington. All of the stores were located on the interstates, and although some were bigger than what Love's had been building, all were quickly rebranded and restocked. When added to the fourteen new stores

If the company he and Judy had founded was going to survive and prosper, they had to constantly seek greater efficiencies, work better as a team with a unified vision, and ceaselessly search for the next opportunity to launch a new trajectory of growth.

then under construction, the Love's chain grew to 260 stores in thirty-eight states in 2010.

After forty-six years in business, starting from one leased service station in Watonga, Oklahoma, Love's Travel Stops & Country Stores had grown into an industry leader with a footprint that stretched from coast to coast. Tom Love, as the foremost agent of that growth, was proud of what his team had accomplished. Still, he was not yet satisfied.

He knew that growth added pressure to operating systems, and he knew that the marketplace and competitors would continue changing all around them while they were on the move. If the company he and Judy had founded was going to survive and prosper, they had to constantly seek greater efficiencies, work better as a team with a unified vision, and ceaselessly search for the next opportunity to launch a new trajectory of growth. As his company approached its semi-centennial birthday, Tom increasingly used one of his favorite metaphors to express his concerns:

"Yesterdays trophies don't win tomorrow's games."

With growth into new parts of the country, Love's needed ways to brand the company beyond the look and performance of stores. Sponsorship on the NASCAR circuit reached a national audience and appealed to road warriors making their living in eighteen wheelers.

Like the hub on a wagon wheel, the headquarters team in Oklahoma City was the pressure point where all the moving pieces of the puzzle came together. If there were weaknesses at the core, the people on the front lines might perform on pride and energy for a short time, but ultimately they would suffer from lack of direction and a breakdown in teamwork.

In 2010, that core was stronger than ever, even as the wheel turned at a faster speed. Tom Love, who had been chief executive officer and chairman of the board since the beginning, was still engaged in every major decision, but he increasingly relied on Greg, Frank, and Jenny to carry the daily load of family ownership. Each had their own individual strengths and talents, but together, they forged a seamless hub that provided a unified vision as a map to the future.

The top management group reflected that teamwork. On any given day, strong willed veterans like Tom Edwards and Doug Stussi might disagree on a particular issue, but once they presented their best arguments and the family owners reached a decision, they were on point ready to lead their respective teams. At each level of management outward, from division and district managers to general managers, the delegation of authority encouraged individual initiative as long as the unified goals remained consistent.

Leadership, alone, was not enough at the hub of the organiza-

Looking to the future, the Love's leadership team has strengthened support services with new corporate office buildings (below) and the inclusion of third generation family members in company culture. With Tom and Greg (facing past) are Greg's sons, Thomas (left) and David (right).

tion. There had to be support for team members on the front line of customer service, whether it was information needed to make good decisions and maintain control or the tools to increase efficiency and keep costs at the lowest possible margin. The accounting department provides a good example of how that centralized support evolved.

The original accounting department in 1964 was one person, Judy Love, who kept books, paid invoices, and prepared profit and loss statements, all by hand in a ledger. For years, even after she left day-to-day operations to complete college, accounting duties were parceled out to a number of desks that included administrative assistants to the top managers. By 2004, the accounting department still had only thirty employees to support 159 Country Stores and

Travel Stops and the start-up enterprises of Musket and Gemini.

Two changes exposed the inadequacy of this small support team. One was the increased emphasis on operational efficiencies, from purchasing and inventory control to invoices and reporting, that needed a steady and accurate stream of information. The other was the growing success of both Gemini trucking and Musket whole-sale fuel distribution, which exceeded the proportional growth in the number of stores in the race to go coast to coast. From 2004 to 2008, as the number of stores climbed from 159 to 204, the number of quarterly invoices generated by Musket alone exploded to 9,000 in 2006, 23,000 in 2007, and 54,000 in 2008, a 500 percent increase in only two years. The only way to manage that increased volume of work was a larger accounting staff, which grew to 75 in 2006 and 115 in 2007. Other support teams such as dispatch, fuel trading, real estate, construction, human resources, and information technology had to keep pace with the expanding operational network.

In the early 1980s, when all of the central staff working for Tom Love, Larry Dillard, Lindell Pearson, and Paula Downing could fit into one small building, they built the first company-owned head-quarters at the southwest corner of Hefner Road and Pennsylvania Avenue in Oklahoma City. In 1993, to accommodate a larger staff,

Less than five years later, the phenomenal growth of the company forced yet another expansion of the headquarters campus. In 2012, work began on a new building west of the existing headquarters.

Staff members joined the Love family, including (left to right) Jenny, Tom, Judy, and Greg, at the dedication of the new headquarters addition in Oklahoma City.

they simply tore out all the walls and converted much of the space to an open floor plan with modular work stations. Subsequent growth in the staff was met by leasing space in nearby buildings.

That makeshift strategy was not working well by 2006. There were simply too many people trying to coordinate an increasingly complex business plan from too many places. Tom Love and the family decided to build a second building. It was two-stories tall, with 31,000 square feet of space, located to the north of the original building. It included a reception lobby, a round board room, eight conference rooms, and special features such as a fitness room and tornado-proof space for computer equipment. The new building opened in the spring of 2007 with a courtyard and water feature connecting it to the original headquarters.

Less than five years later, the phenomenal growth of the company forced yet another expansion of the headquarters campus. In 2012, work began on a new building west of the existing headquarters with a ground-breaking ceremony led by Jenny Love Meyer and twelve of the longest tenured employees, including Harold Wells, who had been with the company since 1973. The new four-story building would have 65,000 square feet of space, enough for 400 employees. Before it was finished, it was already deemed too small.

Along with leadership and support, the headquarters staff in Oklahoma City provided a growing arsenal of tools used by Love's employees on the front lines of customer service. At its earliest and simplest levels, Tom Love had found used mechanical gas pumps for his first service stations in 1964. Thereafter, the challenges grew ever more complex, whether it was an indoor switch to control gas pumps or a cash register that tabulated daily totals. To control labor costs and create efficiencies, new tools became the weapons of progress.

The big leap forward came with the age of computers. First came credit card readers on every pump in 1993, followed two years later by the installation of computer work stations in all Love's. For cashiers, the new computers tracked sales, inventory, purchases, and daily totals. For general managers, the work stations automated personnel records and streamlined daily and weekly reports. For district, divisional, and corporate managers, the flow of information offered greater control and improved the decision-making process.

Jim Xenos, who had come to Love's with Tom Edwards in 1997, steadily expanded the use of technology to save money and provide better customer service. One of his most ambitious projects was the installation of a new point-of-sale system called Retalix. Started in 2007 and completed within a year, it was what Xenos called an "end to end solution" to the control of information that integrated the commercial

The courtyard of the expanded headquarters building included a sculpture that expressed Tom's interest in wildlife conservation and patriotism.

fuel desk into the main cashier system. "All team members will have one single point of sales system for every transaction," said Xenos, "whether they are in the store, in the restaurant, or at the fuel desk."

Two years later, Xenos and his team followed with a hand-held mobile device called DAX, which gave team members access to the Relatix system from anywhere in the store. "From one access point," he said, "managers can see the real-time position and activity of every function in the company by item, category, and store." The new tool tracked the shelf life of goods, which helped reduce waste, and alerted managers when stocks were short, which helped keep shelves stocked.

Technology was just as useful outside the stores in the never ending search for reduced costs and greater efficiencies. At the pumps, a new system using radio frequency identifiable readers was installed so trucks with Love's fuel tags would begin the fuel transaction the moment they pulled in. The new tool replaced billing cards, reduced the time needed for fueling, and cut down on stolen fuel. Farther afield, the team launched Love's Connect, a mobile application for smartphones that led customers to the nearest store, provided information such as the cost of fuel, and offered special deals and rewards. Jerry Hamm, Love's marketing manager, called the new program "a loyalty-building tool."

Although technology could do wonders for efficient operations, there was no substitute for a well trained and motivated work force on the front lines of service in the stores. Tom Edwards, who had helped shape a vigorous management team at the division, district, and store levels, admitted that the biggest challenge to quality service and long term progress was finding good hourly employees. "We need to work on what we think is going to create a good working environment," he said in one interview. "If we continue to foster that environment, we should be the employer of choice."

The Love's team relied on two key strategies to recruit and retain hourly workers. Benefits were important to attract quality applicants, but the ability to retain and grow leaders was based on upward mobility, both in any given store and throughout the expanding system. At a Travel Stop or Country Store, an hourly worker might start on a cash register, work his or her way up to shift leader, and earn increased responsibility as a marketing manager.

Roxie Walker started working as a cashier at the Love's in Richmond, Louisiana, in 2001. Within eight years she advanced to a shift manager, an administrative assistant, and marketing manager. "I've tried to take on more responsibilities and learn everything that goes on in the store," she said in an interview. Phil Sothen was seventeen years old in 2005 when he joined the Love's in Zanesville, Ohio, as an

> Like the vision driving the company's growth, willingness to help others began at the top with the family owners.

Arby's crew member. Within six years, he became a restaurant team member, restaurant shift leader, and store shift leader. "At Love's they help you accomplish anything you want," he said. "You can move up as quickly as you want if you're wiling to work hard and follow all the company policies."

Yessica Martinez, a recent graduate from high school, found encouragement on all sides. From a distance, the Love family created an incentive for personal growth in 2011 with a new college scholarship program that provided up to $2,000 a year to part time students and $4,000 for those who could balance full time college with their jobs. Beverly Obel-Jorgensen, a fellow employee at the Love's Travel Stop in Lost Hills, California, provided more immediate encouragement. Beverly, who had started her own career as a cashier and moved up the career ladder to be the manager of an in-store Arby's, told Yessica, "you can work your way up at Love's because there is room to grow, but you have to keep focused on the goal." Within three years, Yessica became a shift leader and then an assistant manager in the Arby's, all by the time she was twenty-one years old. "We all get along," she said, "it's like a second family."

The family metaphor, which had long been used to describe the team spirit at Love's, became an official pledge when the company

Tom and Judy Love clearly saw the expanded headquarters as another tool to sustain Love's reputation for "the cheapest fuel in town" with "clean places, friendly places." The store over their shoulders is located on the southwest corner of Hefner Road and Pennsylvania Avenue in Oklahoma City.

leadership adopted the phrase, "Making a difference: You take care of your customers and we will take care of you." The benefits package offered to all employees, whether in management or in the hourly ranks, started growing in 1995 with a 401K plan that matched fifty percent of an employee's contribution to their retirement fund up to five percent of wages. An additional benefit was health care insurance, with the company covering seventy-five percent of the cost. In 2009, that contribution amounted to an average of $5,800 for every employee who enrolled in the group health plan.

In 2010, the Love family expanded the safety net with a new program that provided employees with financial emergency assistance. There had long been an informal understanding that an employee facing a crisis could get help either from their co-workers or from the company, but the process lacked structure and consistency. LEEF, short for Love's Employee Emergency Fund, increased the budget allocation for assistance and created a committee of employees who would consider needs and make recommendations on how to help. When Jenny Love Meyer announced the new initiative in the company newsletter, she expressed the spirit of the plan for her co-workers: "We hope that none of you ever experience a tragedy, but if you do, LEEF–and Love's–will be there for you."

The spirit of taking care of one another did not stop at the curb of a Love's Travel Stop or Country Store. It permeated all levels of the company, from the Love family to team members scattered from coast to coast, and included both one-time donations for special needs and structured campaigns that helped others and fostered a sense of unity within the Love's organization. Like the vision driving the company's growth, that willingness to help others began at the top with the family owners.

A sense of service was a family tradition for Tom Love. Two of his uncles were priests, as was his oldest brother and first cousin. His niece is a nun. His father was a civic leader who served as a reform-minded member of the Oklahoma City governing council. Setting the pace, however, was Tom's mother, Margaret, whose life revolved around family, church, and serving the community.

In a newspaper article published in 1968, a reporter needed more than 400 words to describe Margaret's volunteer work. "Mrs. Love has so many demands on her time, you'd think she'd need a computer to keep track of where she needs to be...among other things, she's done volunteer work for the United Fund, the Oklahoma City Symphony, the Art Center League, the Association for Responsible Government, and the Traveler's Aid." The reporter added

Tom's niece, Sister Amy Marie of Jesus, a member of the order of Little Sisters of the Poor.

After the beginning of the new century, Frank noticed a natural transition in the Love family's relationship with employees across the country. As he and Greg made their visits to stores, the employees regularly asked, "How's Tom?" followed by "Where's Jenny?"

Tom's mother, Margaret Love (above and facing page), set an example of community service to her sons, (from left to right) Jack Love, Charles Love, Margaret, Tom, and William Love.

her own opinion: "Obviously, she's a pretty good organizer because she also finds time to study art, take adult education courses, read, knit, cook, and work outdoors."

Margaret's passion for service was carried on by her daughter-in-law, Judy Love. As she and Tom were building a company and raising four children, Judy spent much of her time in church and civic involvement. She chaired boards for Bishop McGuinness High School and St. Ann Nursing Home. She did all the design and decorating for St. Ann, Catholic Charities Home for Redeeming Love, and Archbishop Charles Salatka's home at the Archdiocesan Center, using most of the furniture and art work from the historic Bishop's mansion. She was also very involved with St. Anthony Hospital and Christ the King Church, among many other civic endeavors, as well as being part of the donation committee for Love's and serving as corporate secretary. To provide a formal structure to their giving, Judy and Tom established the Love Family Foundation in 1999 and the Tom and Judy Love Foundation in 2013.

The Love family shared their sense of community service with their employees. For years, the crew at each new store selected a recipient for a $2,000 gift to be announced at the time of opening. When a Country Store opened in Hooker, Oklahoma, in 2009, the employees gave their money to new lights for an American Legion baseball field. In Post Falls, Idaho, the employees gave their money to the Boys and Girls Club of Lootenai County.

To celebrate the team effort that had built Love's, the family allocated $450 to each store to give to a local non-profit organization as the company celebrated its 45th Anniversary in 2008. The only stipulations were that the organization worked to improve the community, and preference should be given to education, youth programs, and health-related causes. At company headquarters in Oklahoma City, every employee was granted similar control over a $450 donation to be made during a campaign called "Making a Difference from the Heart." Oklahoma City Mayor Mick Cornett, prefacing his remarks with a comment about the economic crisis sweeping the globe, offered this observation: "I can assure you that Love's generosity will have a direct, positive impact on the ability of local non-profit organizations to serve our community...It will make a difference–a big one."

Sharing the joy of giving with all employees coast to coast was central to a recurring effort each September to raise money for Children's Miracle Network Hospitals, co-founded by music and television star Marie Osmond. Beginning in 1998, when Love's became a sponsor, each store competed against other stores, but the money raised went to one of the 170 hospitals closest to their community.

That first year, more than $20,000 was raised. Everyone in the organization, from top to bottom, thought they could do better.

The friendly competition was both an effective fund-raising method and a recurring team-building exercise. Kenneth Riggs, a district manager in Arkansas and Tennessee, motivated his co-workers with clear goals and memorable follow-up. "I think it is our responsibility to step in when we are needed," he told his crews. "Raising money for CMN Hospitals is important because the funds we raise go to help sick children...they don't ask for their situation and cannot help themselves...somebody else has to do it." Before each campaign, Kenneth took his store managers on a tour of either the Arkansas Children's Hospital in Little Rock, Arkansas, or LeBonheur Hospital in Memphis, Tennessee, to show the results of their teamwork.

Individual store crews became more creative each year as the annual campaign grew. In 2011, at the Love's Country Store in Okemah, Oklahoma, the employees asked customers for small donations and organized weekly activities such as bake sales, car washes, spaghetti dinners, dunk tanks, a silent auction, and local cheerleaders pumping gas in exchange for donations. Other teams responded with similar creativity. The crew working at a Love's Travel Stop in Palestine, Arkansas, staged a cookout with live music featuring the

One of the largest items raffled to benefit the Children's Miracle Network Hospitals was a car. The car was decorated with the Children's Miracle Network hearts that were sold in store locations.

(Above) Tom and Judy Love with bronze plaque at the dedication of Margaret's Garden made possible by the Love Family, St. Anthony's Hospital, September, 2006.

(Facing page) Tom Love, inducted into the Oklahoma Hall of Fame in 2000, served as Presenter for Judy Love upon her induction in 2010. Together, the couple has received an additional six civic awards, with Tom being recognized with nine individual civic and national awards and Judy receiving eleven individual civic awards. In addition, Tom has served as chairman of the Oklahoma Transportation Commission, Oklahoma Business Roundtable, and Trust Coalition. Judy has chaired or co-chaired twelve major civic events and served on thirteen civic boards.

(Below) Barbara Brou and Judy Love, co-chairs of the Oklahoma City Heart Ball benefiting the American Heart Association.

general manager on guitar. Two managers at the Love's in Buckeye, Arizona, pledged to shave their heads if their team raised $11,000, with the shearing honors given to the top two fund raisers. Michael Young, the general manager at a Love's in Oklahoma City, was featured on local television for wearing a dress an entire work day to get more donations. From 1998 through 2013 Love's store teams raised more than $10-million for Children's Miracle Network Hospitals.

Whether it was providing the cheapest gas in town or making a difference in the life of a child, the people of Love's proved that working together could foster a sense of family.

As the company he and Judy founded in 1964 approached its semi-centennial birthday, Tom Love was still thinking about the future. "Most companies follow a bell curve," he told this author in one early interview as he stood in front of a chalk board emphasizing the importance of his message with bold strokes. "They start with entrepreneurial vigor down here, grow as people come together with a shared vision, and mature on a plateau when the original business plan reaches its peak...then they start a slow descent as they reap the rewards of earlier investment and competitors with fresh ideas push them aside...at Love's, we have to avoid that slow descent." If "Clean Places, Friendly Faces" had become the external brand for the company, "Yesterday's trophies don't win tomorrow's games" had become the internal mantra of what Tom Love expected both from himself and those around him.

Like a veteran coach who assembles a team and approves a game plan, Tom had surrounded himself with good people em-

To counterbalance the challenges of being spread coast to coast, the company turned to an internal trucking fleet (right) while top executives turned to jets (facing page) as the most efficient way to maintain personal relationships with managers and team members in the stores.

powered with the responsibility to cope with challenges and seize opportunities. In 2008, as faith in the economy was shaken by the crash of the Great Recession, they launched a new enterprise called Tire Care Centers, open twenty-four hours a day providing Michelin truck tires, road-side assistance, lube services, and minor repairs. Within five years, there were more than 170 Love's Tire Centers scattered from coast to coast. In 2010, after one of their most aggressive competitors filed for bankruptcy in the wake of the Great Recession, the Love's team pushed doubt aside and purchased twenty-six truck stops and expanded into four key new states overnight. The next year, they made a leap of faith and invested in more than a dozen fueling stations offering compressed natural gas, a fuel of the future which was equally good for the environment, the country, and their customers.

Coping with challenges and seizing opportunities alone, however, were not enough to avoid the pitfalls that pulled most companies into decline. Shared vision and teamwork, Tom knew, were critical if they were going to match ambition with execution, and at the heart of shared vision and teamwork was communication. If Love's was going to find new trajectories of growth, the team had to be on the same page pushing and pulling the same direction.

In the short term, Tom knew his three children in the ownership circle would keep the momentum going with effective communication among themselves and with their co-workers throughout the ranks of the company from top to bottom. In the long term, they had to make sure that unity of vision and action would be embraced by the third generation of the Love family. Several of Tom's and Judy's grandchildren were already serving internships at the company, just beginning the learning process that would prepare them for future responsibilities.

Tom knew that same sense of dynamic change was needed to keep the ranks of management strong. He had built the company by finding the right people at the right time, whether they rose from the ranks or came to Love's with skills and ambition. To constantly prime that pump, Tom and his leadership team maintained a grueling schedule of business reviews that bridged the gap between headquarters leadership and the frontline team members in the field. The only concession Tom had made to the march of time was substituting travel by private jet for his beloved travel by car. After forty-nine and a half years in the business, Tom Love was still the road warrior.

At one time, Tom had known everyone in the company. Those days are long gone, victim to success and the growth of the Love's team to more than 11,000 people scattered at more than 300 stores coast to coast. To partially satisfy his craving for connection to his co-workers, he and Jenny initiated a series called "Talks with Tom." This author was allowed to attend the third installment on May 22, 2013.

Eighteen people from the headquarters staff were seated at the round board table when Tom arrived sharply at 1:00 pm. Jenny rose and explained that "Talks with Tom" was another way to keep in touch and ask questions. With a stroke of understatement, she added, "I think everyone here knows my Dad." There were smiles all around as he rose to speak.

He started with a story to illustrate how much the company had grown. "I recently attended a meeting with a group of co-workers in the field when I heard one young man ask his general manager, 'who's the dude in the tie?' The company has grown so much, we need to get to know each other." He then asked each of them

Jenny addressed colleagues at a new initiative she called "Talks with Tom." Tom, standing to her right, used these intimate meetings to encourage communication up and down the chain of command.

around the table to introduce themselves and describe their work. His pride in their descriptions was interrupted only by his occasional comments, such as "you are one of the Sizzle Sisters" or "you are the actor I have heard about."

Over the next hour, Tom answered questions without hesitation, especially when it involved growth, his favorite topic. He analyzed the benefits of adding tire centers, used specific numbers to illustrate the advantages of fuel-by-rail opportunities, and admitted they were considering an experiment with lodging at some of their remote locations. He talked about core values, integrity, and momentum. When asked about aid for stricken families suffering from the recent tornado that struck Moore, Oklahoma, he said he and the family were gathering that afternoon to discuss it. Within days, when everyone in the room learned they decided to give $3 million to relief, they felt like they had been part of the conversation.

Finally, one person in the room asked Tom how he felt about the approaching fiftieth birthday of the company. He paused briefly as if gathering his thoughts, then said, "It's hard to see great change year to year, but I can see it decade to decade. It takes a long time to get anything done well and the people and skills to build a company take a long time to gather and get on the same page."

After another pause, he looked around the room at those gathered with him and said, "I will let Bob Blackburn look at the last fifty years...I will look at the next fifty years."

He added, "Yesterday's trophies don't win tomorrow's games."

RECALIBRATE AND RELOAD

Tom did not take long to act on his promise to look ahead.

   With the company's history still fresh on everyone's minds, he issued a bold challenge to his family and team leaders. "It has taken us fifty years to build this company to its current size," he said. "Let's double it by 2020, only six years away, and while we are accomplishing that, let's maintain the historic annual balance of at least sixteen percent net operating profit, protect our company's culture, and keep Love's a family-owned enterprise."

Facing page: Tom Love and Jenny Love Meyer celebrated on stage at the 50th Anniversary Gala to commemorate the founding of Love's Travel Stops and Country Stores.

In one meeting, set against the backdrop of a successful past, the ground rules were laid for an eventful future.

Throughout the history of Love's, growth had been woven into the very fabric of the company. Growth, above all, created upward mobility that would help them recruit top talent, retain those willing to lead, and reward those who converted lessons learned into practice and performance. And with a growing leadership team would come innovation, blending new ideas into proven strategies, allowing people to make mistakes, encouraging everyone to learn. "Success in our business is all about the people," emphasized Jenny Love Meyer.

In real numbers, the challenge was daunting. For years, the average number of stores opened each year ranged from ten to twelve, and occasionally dropped below that. If they were to double the size of the company by 2020, it would mean averaging thirty-five to forty new stores a year, doubling the number of employees scattered from coast to coast, and embracing time-consuming changes along the way as the marketplace continued to evolve. "The rate of the proposed expansion might have killed another organization," remembered Kevin Asbury, a thirty-year veteran of the company, "but it was just second nature to us."

In the company newsletter sent to all employees, the Love family simplified the strategy for reaching the goal. "In addition to focusing on the customer," said Greg, "the three most important pieces to our business are people, product, and capital." The family had always pointed with pride to the generation of leaders who had come into the company in the late 1990s, and they were encouraged by the next crop of leaders who were starting to make their mark.

They also liked the vertical diversification that was still in its infancy. "All of our component parts," Frank added, "have to harmonize." And finally, they emphasized that securing the right financials to keep the company private was critical. "I fully expect

Tom and Judy Love in November, 2014 (facing page).

that Love's will be family owned for as far out as I can imagine," said Tom, "because it works."

For Tom Love, his family and his co-workers, the road to success would be steep and slippery, filled with challenges that would test them all.

While Love's leadership team preferred to keep their focus on internal efficiencies and profitability to drive expansion, they knew their goal of doubling the number of stores faced a major challenge from competition. One side of that challenge was acquiring locations on highways with enough car and truck traffic to support a travel stop. There was only so much real estate to go around, and the city-to-city interstate system had been completed in the 1970s. The other battlefront was the fight for market share. In 1964, when Tom and Judy launched their first filling station, they used "the cheapest gas in town" to compete with their local rivals. In 2014 the competitive challenge was spread across a diverse mix of products at any one location and included lean, highly motivated local independent operators and national chains with deep resources and scales of economy.

In 2014 more than 75 percent of all truck stops in the United States were owned by local independent operators. Some, like Iowa 80, relied on size and extra services to attract customers and gain market share. Founded in 1964 along the banks of the Mississippi River, Iowa 80 was described in the press as a "Truckers' Disneyland" with eight restaurants, a convenience store, gift shop, Super Truck Showroom, barber shop, chiropractor, dentist, movie theater, work out room, laundry, mechanical service, truck wash, pet grooming, and twenty-four private showers. Another creative local competitor was the Russell family with two travel centers in New Mexico, one of which was on the lucrative Interstate 40 corridor. Russell's Travel Centers offered competitive prices for diesel and gasoline, but pulled customers in with the usual amenities plus a 1950's-style dining room and first class car museum with free admission.

While outflanking local independent competitors, the Love's team went head to head across the continent with two major truck stop operators. One was Travel Centers of America, which included the merged brands of TA, Petro, and Petro Stopping Centers. When Tom threw down his challenge of doubling the size of Love's, TA/Petro had more than 250 locations in 43 states with more than

24,000 employees. Most importantly, they had many of the prime real estate locations on the interstate highway system.

While TA/Petro was handicapped by venture-funded corporate ownership, Pilot/Flying J had grown with a business plan similar to that at Love's with family ownership and long term strategies. Founded in 1958 with one gas station in Virginia, it grew under the Haslam family to more than 600 locations across North America with more than 27,000 employees and annual revenue exceeding $20 billion. The business plan, locations, and leadership impressed Warren Buffett enough that he would buy a 38.6 percent share of the company in 2017 with plans to be the biggest shareholder in six years with 80 percent ownership.

Another challenge facing Tom and his team was the changing face of the trucking industry, the single largest source of income at any travel stop. After the national recession hit bottom in 2009, the trucking industry entered a phase of aggressive acquisitions and consolidation. High labor costs squeezed profit margins; fuel costs

Tom and Greg Love joined Herb Bowman in 2014 to celebrate the expansion into the hotel business just as Tom was challenging his leadership team to double the size of the company in six years.

soared; and the price of new, high-tech equipment rose to historic levels. Other factors driving consolidation included the retirement of independent operators who entered the industry in the early 1980s and the growth of super-sized companies needing coast-to-coast shipping.

From 2014 to 2018, a series of acquisitions rocked the industry. The biggest deal was the merger of Swift Transportation Co., the sixth-largest trucking company in the country, and Knight Transportation Inc., the 23rd largest. The combined value of the new firm was estimated at $5 billion. XPO Logistics, a former

Oklahoma Supreme Court Justice Steven W. Taylor swore-in Greg Love as a member of the Oklahoma Transportation Commission, a gubernatorial appointment that reflected Love's leadership in the trucking and travel industries.

176

brokerage firm, used a war chest of more than $8 billion to go on a buying binge for struggling transport firms such as Conway. "For many family-owned truck companies," wrote one reporter, "their options are to sell out or shut down." The Love's team, which had found a niche on the interstate highways with owner-operators in 1981, had to adjust to the changing marketplace while launching its accelerated expansion.

Consolidation was not the only challenge facing travel stop operators. Congress passed the first fuel efficiency standards for heavy duty trucks in 2011. With fuel costs making up 25 percent of all operating expenses, truck fleets were already adopting changes to increase mileage. By 2017 fleets had improved fuel efficiency every year for eight straight years and it was projected that three percent increases a year were just around the corner. For truck stop operators, that meant sales volume would decrease another three percent a year even with the same number of customers.

Another factor changing the trucking industry was electronic logging devices mandated by the federal government. When drivers kept paper logs of their hours on the road, it was easy to manipulate the system and drive more than the maximum eleven hours a day. With electronic logging going into effect by 2017, violations would be easy to catch with severe penalties. Paid only when their tires were turning, drivers increasingly put a premium on truck stops that could get them into and out of fueling bays safely and quicker and provide services such as tires, repairs, food, showers, and equipment during one quick stop. And with restricted time on the road, drivers needed more parking places where they could rest between shifts.

On top of these external challenges to expansion were the internal risks of growth, such as the impact on span of control, flexible capital investment funds, and recruiting and retaining quality team members. Prior to 1981, when Love's was a compact system of Country Stores spread across three states, Tom, Lindell Pearson, and Larry Dillard could drive to each location, observe operations, and keep a close eye on quality. In the 1990s, with Love's Travel Stops opening well beyond regional reach with a growing list of profit centers, Tom brought in Tom Edwards to create a badly needed span of control. If the system was to double yet again, new tools for communication and control would be critical in the struggle to protect the company's brand.

Financing the expansion would be just as tricky. In the days of the Country Stores, Tom and Judy could borrow money from country bankers in the towns where they were willing to create new

As the Love's organization launched the effort to double the size of the company in six years, one of the greatest assets was the Love family, including Greg and his family (above) and Jenny and her family (below).

Frank and his family (above) and Laura and her family (below).

jobs and add to the local community. Once they expanded to the interstate highways with no local incentives, they relied on cash flow and lease-back financing. If the company was to expand by thirty-five or forty stores a year, they would need enough capital to seize opportunities and react quickly in a marketplace where competition did not favor the slow and timid. A more sophisticated capital formation strategy would need to be developed.

Most importantly, the expansion would test the ability to recruit, train, and retain a growing work force. More stores would mean more team members, three shifts per store, more managers with the work ethic and potential for leadership, and a unified management team that shared a common vision, spoke with one voice, and understood their role on a team that was constantly tackling new challenges and chasing new opportunities. As Tom Edwards constantly reminded everyone on his team, "it is all about the people." If the company was going to double in size in six years, the greatest challenge of all would come down to the ability to recruit, train, and retain a work force that could live up to and exceed the standards set during the first fifty years of the company's history.

It was time to get to work.

Of all the assets needed for the challenges ahead, the most critical was the leadership team, which started at the top with the Love family. Tom, still as enthusiastic about the company's future as he ever had been, was executive chairman and a daily inspiration to everyone around him. After fifty years in the industry, he had a deep well of experience to draw from and share.

Taking on an ever increasing load of day-to-day leadership duties were three of Tom's and Judy's children. Greg and Frank, both veterans of the industry with more than fifty years of combined experience, served as co-chief executive officers. Jenny joined the company in the early 1990s, and like her brothers, started as a manager and worked her way up to vice president. Although the family spoke with one voice in major decisions, Greg tended to focus on development initiatives such as construction, Frank specialized in operations, logistics, and fuel trading, and Jenny devoted most of her time to communications and culture. Laura, the second-born child, may not have carved out a specialty on the management team, but she was fully engaged in family discussions affecting the welfare of the company. Judy, at Tom's side since the very beginning, served as the family matriarch with a watchful eye on philanthropy and community engagement.

The Loves considered the senior leadership team an extension of their own family. "We've been on the same team a long time," observed Frank Love, "and these managers have a track record of success, which gives us confidence in their decisions." That confidence, itself, was an asset in an industry where people had to make quick decisions in the heat of battle, whether it was responding to competitors or recognizing opportunities. "Our confidence in the team allows us to empower them to make a lot of decisions that have to creep up the corporate ladder in other companies," said Frank. "The ability to get things done here is exceptional."

Contributing to that efficiency was an organizational structure that was relatively flat compared to other companies with a footprint that stretched from coast to coast. There were self-contained support units, such as fuel acquisition, transportation, accounting, human resources, and finance that helped grease the wheels of efficiency, but the greatest contributor to the span of control was on the operational side of delivering services to the traveling public. There, on the front lines of attracting, serving, and keeping customers, the Love's team faced its greatest challenge of achieving a net operating profit of at least 16 percent and preserving the brand while the company expanded.

At the front of this management team was the executive vice president of operations, a position that was redefined in the 1990s by Tom Edwards. Serving alongside that critical position were two vice presidents of operations, one at the top of the management team to the east and one to the west. Reporting to them were eight divisional directors and fifty district managers, considered by many in the organization to be the most critical positions in the entire company. Each district manager supervised eight to twelve stores, each with a general manager, restaurant manager, tire care manager, and team members in customer service. Up and down this organizational structure, the three keys to success were finding the right people, delivering exceptional service, and paying attention to detail.

It had long been part of Love's culture for the management team to look for talented people who would be capable of running the company ten to fifteen years in the future. Some in leadership had started at the store level, and through proven results, risen through the ranks. Others, recruited with specific skills needed on

Kevin Asbury, who had worked his way up the leadership ladder at Love's, was named executive vice president of operations as the effort to double the size of the company gained momentum.

the team, had joined Love's in mid-career. Just as the momentum was building in the race to double the size of the company, the top managers in operations represented that combination of home-grown talent and selective recruitment.

When Tom Edwards accepted the challenge of starting a new tire care venture for the Love family, Kevin Asbury was ready to step into that role as executive vice president of operations. Kevin, a native of Kansas, was recruited on his college campus and served as a store manager for two years, a district manager for ten years, a divisional director for four years, and vice president of human resources for another five years. As Greg Love would later recall, "Kevin had done it all. He knew the company from ground up, and most importantly, he understood the heat of fire at the store level."

Kevin also had the right personal style for the coming challenge of doubling the size of the company in six years. "Kevin is a problem solver," said Greg. "He is a good listener, a collaborator, who is empathetic with the challenges of what we throw at operations personnel, whether it is a district manager trying to keep the leadership pipeline well stocked or a general manager trying to stay on top of the slightest details." In the years after starting the grand expansion, Kevin continued to evolve the operating model to meet the changing business challenges. With more complexity than ever before due not only to explosive growth but also the increased demands of the Love's Tire and Truck Care business, Kevin was able to lean on his strengths and winning track record to make sure that every general manager and district manager was set up for success.

The two vice presidents working with Kevin had taken different paths to leadership. Roger Ahuja, the son of a scientist with the USDA, grew up in California and Hawaii, but graduated from college in Durant, Oklahoma with a degree in accounting. He started his career with Taco Bell, where he was managing several stores when Carl Martincich recruited him to Love's in 1994. Within a year, quicker than normal, Roger was asked to open a new Loves' Travel Stop in Texas.

Roger's career path prepared him well for each new step. He ran a training store for restaurant managers, served as a district manager for Country Stores, and was a district manager in 1997 when Tom Edwards was brought in to reorganize operations. Roger embraced the new system and quickly recognized the advantages of structured repetition. Years later, looking back on that turning point, Roger summarized the changes. "Every visit to a store was structured," he said, "with key performance indicators that gave us coaching opportunities to help younger employees. Disciplined people with disciplined plans and disciplined actions led to disciplined results." In 2015 Roger was named vice president of operations for the western half of the United States.

Taking a different path to vice president of operations in the eastern half of the country was Gary Price. A native of Delaware, Gary worked his way through college on an ROTC scholarship, earned a degree in accounting, and joined the U.S. Army in time to serve as a ranger in the first Gulf War. Along with many junior officers, he left the military during cutbacks in funding. He was recruited by PepsiCo and specialized in food service before joining Pilot Travel Centers, where he rose to division director of the West Coast and vice president of food service. After a brief stint as president for a restaurant chain, he interviewed with Love's and became a division director out of Nashville, Tennessee. Within a year and a half, again quicker than normal, he was promoted to vice president of operations.

Both Roger and Gary described their roles on the leadership team as marching into battle shoulder to shoulder with division

Roger Ahuja, seen here with two Love's employees at a training event, was named vice president of operations in the western half of the country in 2015.

Gary Price, a veteran who had served his country in the First Gulf War, joined Love's as a division director and was quickly promoted to vice president of operations for the eastern half of the country.

directors to serve their district managers, each of whom was responsible for six to eight stores with 400 to 500 employees and sales that often exceeded three quarters of a billion dollars. "That's where the rubber meets the road," said Gary Price. "In addition to gaining efficiencies, the district managers are in charge of developing talent that keeps the pipeline of leadership filled with quality candidates."

The leadership pipeline started with assistant managers, who went through positional training to learn how to manage each station, from registers and food service to tire shops and maintenance. After ten weeks of basic training, said Gary, the new recruits were "given the keys to run a shift and told to not burn the building down." The next steps were to become an operations manager running a shift and then a general manager in charge of the entire store. After a year as general manager, they became candidates for district manager positions based on at least four quarters of proven performance in gross sales, net operating profit, low employee turnover, improved training, and intangibles such as leadership ability and communication skills.

Everyone in the chain of command, from general managers to the Love family, felt the pressure to develop new talent even quicker as the number of new stores accelerated from 2014 to 2018. Each new store needed a proven general manager, a restaurant manager, a tire care manager, and every eight new stores created a new position for a district manager, all while backfilling openings in the management system through normal attrition. To speed the process, the leadership team formalized what had been occasional but successful practices.

In 2007, while still in management at Pilot, Gary Price hired a former military officer named Drew Graham, a native Oklahoman who had gone to West Point and served in the Army as a captain for eight years. With encouragement from Gary, Drew interviewed with Kevin Asbury and was hired to formalize a Junior Officers Program at Love's. "You can train someone to be an accountant," observed Gary Price, "and you can train someone to pull the tactical levels to run the business, but it is difficult to train somebody to be a skilled leader who can inspire others." While Kevin and Gary thought retired military officers could bring those skills to the company, it was a leap of faith and a huge investment by the Love family that would take years to prove its worth.

First, hiring junior military officers leaving the service was a highly competitive pursuit. Big corporations, from General Motors to General Electric, wanted executives who had been trained by some of the best organizations in the world. If Love's wanted to get in that game, they had to hire a specialist head-hunting team to find the candidates, and they had to pay more for a junior officer than they did for a college graduate. Tom Love, a former Marine himself, recognized the risks but liked the potential payback. The bet paid handsomely. By 2018 there were thirty-two former junior and senior military officers working their way up the ranks in the expanding Love's management system.

Another casual recruiting tool converted into a more structured effort to fill leadership positions was the Love's College Internship Program. As early as 2008, corporate staff members in Oklahoma City and Houston were hiring summer interns. Gradually, as the expansion efforts accelerated, the internship program grew into a twelve-week training tool to recruit undergraduates and "give them a snapshot of Love's culture." In 2017 the internship program was expanded to the stores, with seven locations selected based on training opportunities and proximity to universities. From 2008 to 2017, more than fifty interns were hired for full-time jobs with a head start learning the Love's way.

While developing talent from the ground up, the leadership team constantly looked for people outside of Love's who had the right skills, experience, and character to seamlessly join the team. One of those recruits was LaDonna Felder, a native of Mississippi

Jenny Love Meyer visiting with LaDonna Felder, a district manager. Two other female district managers are Mireya Crawford, a 12-year Love's veteran, and Tiffany Sparks, with Love's for 11 years.

Graduates of Love's University, seen here with Tom Love, were an important part of the overall plan to recruit, train, and retain gifted and motivated leaders up and down the management chain of command.

who had worked in the service industry since she was thirteen years old. Her resume included time as a teenaged waitress, a barber, a stint in the Navy, college on the GI Bill, and experience running stores and districts at both Pilot/Flying J and Petro Stopping Centers. In March of 2016, Gary Price, who had recognized LaDonna's skills and work ethic before he left Pilot, recruited her. At first she resisted.

LaDonna had two small children, elderly grandparents, and a church home near the location where she was born. She told Gary she could not be away from her home for long periods. Gary, understanding her situation, told her he had a "monster store" near her hometown that needed a makeover. He also enticed her with the prospect of quickly becoming a district manager with enough stores within a day's drive so she could be home every night. She accepted the offer, saved the store, and became a district manager a year later.

Feeding the leadership team with homegrown and new recruits was only one part of the challenge posed by expansion; the flip side of the story was retaining the best and brightest. As a supplement to a dynamic working environment and pride doing a good job, the best motivation for retention continued to be the Love's Shares program of profit sharing. Under the system, each general manager was eligible to earn two percent of net operating profits at his or her store. District managers, who worked with six or more general managers, could earn a half percent of net profit at his or her stores in their district.

Gemini managers appeard with some of the drivers at an awards ceremony.

To convert their Love's Shares to cash, managers had to stay in the system for seven years, at which time they received an accumulated check. After another three years, they received another check, and thereafter they could get a check every year. In 2018, at the leadership conference in Oklahoma City, more than $20 million in Love's Shares checks were distributed to general and district managers. One district manager received a check for more than $600,000. Not surprisingly, Love's received 400,000 job applications in 2017. Good jobs and fair compensation, combined with opportunities in a rapidly growing company, attracted a steady stream of capable, ambitious people who would become the leaders of the future.

With the leadership pipeline well supplied, it was a race to fulfill Tom's challenge of doubling the size of Love's in six years.

There were two ways for a company like Love's to grow. One was horizontal with more units similar to those that had been built before, enhanced with improvements as the demands of customers changed and lessons were learned. The other was vertical, adding new enterprises to the system that either expanded a particular service or bolted new services onto the existing structure with what Tom Love called "harmony." Both options were expensive, either buying new real estate, building structures, and adding systems or acquiring compatible enterprises with hidden value that would make the entire system more productive. The accelerated pace of growth and innovation put unprecedented demands on access to investment funds.

On the front lines of capitalization were Doug Stussi and Shane Wharton, who had been with the Love's team since the late 1990s. Armed with strong cash flow and a low debt ratio, they assembled a group of capital partners that included a unique combination of local banks, big insurance companies, and national financial giants who respected the transparency and collaborative communication at Love's. "The key to our success in the financial markets is trust," said Shane looking back on their success. "Bankers want to trust the direction management is taking the company and they have to trust the information we are providing."

The long-term relationship with capital partners allowed the company to borrow money at the lowest rates possible, with the greatest flexibility, and the least restrictions on innovation. "We

Recognition for great service to the company was an important aspect of rewarding employees and setting standards for others to follow. Here, Frank Love presented Tiffany Sparks as the recipient of the Founder's Award.

never want to tell the leadership team that we cannot do a deal or seize an opportunity due to lack of fluid capital," said Shane. "And we never want to tell the family that someone is looking over their shoulders with the power to limit their ability to take a risk." As the great expansion began in 2014, Doug and Shane had close working relationships with twelve capital partners providing investment grade financing. Cash would not be a limitation.

The grand expansion also tested leadership's ability to keep pace with the myriad challenges of constructing new stores. It started with selecting sites, a critical factor in success, and extended through contract negotiations, permitting, community relationships, site development, and coordination of materials and building trades. The Love family was confident in the team's ability to meet the challenge in large part due to the leadership of Rick Shuffield, who had started his career with Love's in operations as a division director. In 2002 Greg Love pulled Rick into his development team and gradually gave him increasing responsibilities.

Rick, described by Greg as one of the hardest working leaders at Love's, assembled a team of project managers that reflected his emphasis on team work and detail. By 2018, as the pace of construction increased to an average of three new stores a month, Greg and Rick relied on seven project managers. Half had worked their way up the career ladder at Love's and half had come from the property development industry. Together, they made sure the locations and amenities at every store gave their general managers the greatest chance to succeed.

While the race to doubling the size of the company gained momentum, the Love's team constantly searched for even the slightest competitive advantages. At all stores, especially the Country Stores in small towns, the steady decline in tobacco sales had long challenged their ability to keep sales growing. In response, they filled the gap with a large variety of food offerings such as Godfather's Pizza, SUBWAY sandwiches, and signature coffees.

Proprietary food under the Love's brand was not new, dating to the 1970s with the Fresh Daily Deli, but it was expanded in 2014 with a new program called "Fresh to Go." At each store, one person was assigned the task of buying local produce and preparing fresh fruit cups, vegetable cups, and high quality wrapped sandwiches. The profit margin was higher than pre-packaged foods from vendors and it gave customers greater, healthier options and the chance to save a little time to get back on the road.

On the interstate highways, one of the most important competitive advantages other than price of fuel was still the choice of branded restaurants. New brands were incorporated into the mix, such as Taco John's added in 2016, and SUBWAYs were added to Country Stores in towns of less than 5,000 people. At new Travel Stops, the emerging trend was three restaurants. By 2018 the Love's network of stores included 720 restaurants, with 600 of those managed by Love's employees. The others, including all McDonalds, were operated by franchisees.

While local customers remained important to Country Stores and family motorists remained important to Travel Stops, the most competitive and highly profitable market segment remained the

To expand market share and provide a growing list of services to the trucking industry, the size of Love's stores grew bigger in tandem with the size of the company.

Food was one product where the profit margin could be controlled through creativity. Fresh to Go vegetable and fruit cups were prepared and packaged at the store level.

trucking industry. It was there, on that economic battlefield that the Love's management team looked for competitive advantages and innovations that would attract truckers, increase cash flow per customer, and empower them to double the size of the company in six years. One way to win that battle was to help truck drivers save down time and keep the wheels rolling.

In 2013, just as the effort to double the size of the company was about to begin, Love's was the first travel stop company in the country to offer card-less fueling at every store using radio frequency identification. The system required a secure, low-cost tag placed on the truck's windshield that was detected by a sensor installed in the diesel lanes. The electronic signal turned on the pumps, completed and recorded a secure payment transaction, and shut off the pumps. A similar time-saving innovation was TirePass, implemented in 2015 so a driver could pull into a reserved lane and have a technician inspect the tires, check tire pressure, and record tread depth. By the time fueling was completed, drivers had a written report on tire condition that could help them extend tire life, reduce downtime, and increase fuel efficiency.

Another competitive edge in the battle for truck drivers was the availability of parking spaces. By 2014 there were on average about 1.5 million trucks on the road every day. Each driver was limited to an eleven-hour shift, so at any given time about half of those trucks needed a parking space in the most convenient places with time-saving services close by, but there were only 300,000 to 400,000 parking spaces in the entire country. The truck stop company with the most parking spaces in the best locations with the best services nearby would have a competitive advantage.

As the Love's team accelerated the pace of expansion, the size of new stores grew proportionately with the need for additional services and parking spaces. In 2000 the typical Love's Travel Stop was a 7,000-square-foot building with one restaurant and three showers on eight acres with sixty parking spaces. By 2016 new buildings had stretched to 12,000 square feet with up to three restaurants and seven showers sitting on fifteen acres with 100 parking spaces. "To keep pace with the competition and respond to the needs of truck drivers," reflected Greg Love, "we relied on surveys to pinpoint demand and trusted our general managers to suggest changes that could improve our bottom line."

While the large Travel Stops continued to grow in both numbers and size, the leadership team saw opportunities for smaller stores in locations off the interstate highway system. In 2012, even before the challenge to double the size of the company was issued, existing Country Stores in small towns were undergoing an evolutionary change that included new floors and ceilings, interior wall applications, better lighting, and exteriors with brick or stone. By 2014, when the grand expansion began, they started building new Country Stores in towns of less than 5,000 people. "They are traditional convenience stores," said Kevin Asbury in 2018, "but with modern features, the most current innovations in food service. Our most recent openings were in Garden City, Kansas, Buena Vista, Colorado, and Wynnewood, Oklahoma."

Whether on interstate highways or in small towns, the Love's team knew they could compete successfully in terms of products, services, and quality, but competition tended to reduce profit margins, which in turn threatened the difficult balancing act of 16 percent growth and 16 percent net operating profit. The ongoing battle with TA and Pilot/Flying J for customers on the interstate highways, linked with competition in small towns from local independents, limited the number of locations where a successful store could be built.

To open a new battle front, Tom Love suggested another alternative for expansion off the interstates but on major U.S. highways where there was adequate truck traffic to supplement the local market of commuters and neighborhood customers. There, he reasoned, reduced sales would be offset by avoiding the fierce competition that suppressed profit margins. Internally, the new concept was referred to as Tier 3 stores. "It was Dad's brainchild," recalled Greg Love, "to find locations where we could capture a large market share with our quality amenities, but with a smaller investment in land, structures, and operating expenses."

Typically, each Tier 3 store was to be built on a four-lane

The rapid growth of Love's from 2014 to 2018 offered new opportunities to promote hard working people. Here, Greg and Jenny recognized the good work of Adam Ortiz.

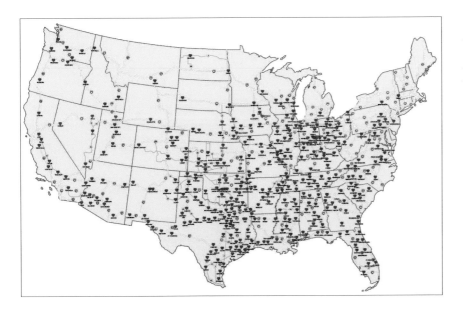

This map of Love's store locations illustrated both market saturation and the complex span of control that tested the leadership team every day.

Brent Bergevin (left), vice president of transportation, joined Greg, Frank, Jenny, and Tom with their management team in front of one of their trucks.

highway either near a major urban center or between pockets of intense industrial activity with both four-wheel and truck traffic. Instead of needing fifteen acres, a building with 12,000 square feet, and 100 truck parking spaces common on an interstate highway, Tier 3 stores needed seven acres, a building with 6,000 square feet, and twenty to thirty truck parking spaces. Other economies of scale include two or three instead of five to seven showers, one instead of two or three restaurants, and a staff of fifteen instead of thirty-five to forty. In early communications with Love's employees, it was emphasized that Tier 3 stores would have "the same amenities as a travel stop but without a truck tire center."

The first Tier 3 store opened in March of 2014 outside of Andrews, Texas, where the oil play was attracting new employees, generating truck traffic twenty-four hours a day, and growing the local economy. Mike Herman, the division director who oversaw the new store, could not contain his enthusiasm when interviewed about the opening. "I'm so excited about this. Every day is like opening a box of candy to me." From the inside looking out, Mike realized that each new store might have less gross sales than a Travel Stop on an interstate highway, but the goal was a 16 percent net operating return on investment while creating new opportunities for training managers in a slower paced environment. From 2014 to 2018, the Love's team would open more than twenty-five Tier 3 stores.

More stores, with more employees, selling more services and

As the Thunder basketball team rose as the national and international brand of Oklahoma City, the company created a "Thunder Tanker" that could share the pride.

products put pressure on support units to keep pace. Musket and Gemini, the company-owned subsidiaries that bought and hauled fuel for the stores, are good examples of the ripple effect of growth. If the system was to double in size in six years, all the while showing a healthy net operating profit, the infrastructure of securing and transporting fuel had to grow as well, especially at Gemini where drivers were increasingly difficult to find and retain.

Brent Bergevin came to Love's as a divisional director and knew how to lead people and processes. Frank Love had chosen him to build Gemini, a huge undertaking dependent on trucks and drivers. He also needed managers who could find the drivers, inspire their teams, and keep a bi-coastal fleet of heavy duty trucks rolling in a profitable and safe way. His command structure started with two division directors, one to the east and one to the west, a manager of logistics, a manager of maintenance and driver compliance, a manager of rail and crude trucking, and a manager of fuel quality. In the field were nineteen regional managers, all of whom had started with Love's as a driver.

The ability to keep every store "wet" was tested every day, especially during natural disasters such as hurricanes. When Hurricanes Harvey and Irma hit the Gulf Coast, the ability to source and deliver fuel was hammered by flooding and loss of electrical power. In Texas the power outage closed refineries, pipelines, and terminals. In Florida the storm closed ports and unloading terminals. To supply fuel to their stores, the buyers at Musket searched for product as far as 300 to 400 miles away from the impacted stores, which stretched the time it took drivers to pick up the fuel and deliver it. At one point in the Dallas/Fort Worth market, one competitor ran out of fuel at 75 percent of its stores, which increased the demand at Love's stores as much as 200 to 300 percent. With only a few short exceptions, the Musket and Gemini teams kept their stores supplied.

In 2011, motivated by both safety and retention of drivers, the Love's team launched the Gemini Safe Driver Credits bonus program. To earn a credit point, drivers had to have no accidents, tickets, or fuel-related incidents for a year, pass all inspections, and receive all quarterly and annual bonuses for a year. Once drivers earned five points, they were eligible to receive a bonus equal to four times their average monthly salary. In 2016, when the first class of eligible drivers hit the five-year minimum time requirement, more than $3.4 million was distributed to 135 drivers. "I'm pleased we have drivers who believe in the system," said Brent at the awards ceremony, "and we've shed blood, sweat, and tears to make this the

As new store openings accelerated to an average of three or four a month, crews demonstrated their pride in a variety of ways. The crew in Beaumont, Texas, formed the shape of a heart.

Although inauspicious looking, this Trillium pump represented a major shift into the compressed natural gas market across the nation.

most driver-focused company possible."

With the lowest turnover rate of drivers in the hazardous materials trucking industry, Gemini handled the expansion challenge with few disruptions in their part of the fuel chain. In 2012 the company had 235 trucks and 547 drivers. Five years later, the numbers had increased to 650 trucks and 1,000 drivers hauling diesel, gasoline, bio diesel, jet fuel, ethanol, crude, and propane. In just one month during the grand expansion, the fleet delivered 56,841 loads of fuel, equivalent to 444,284,672 gallons, while driving 7,437,418 miles. In 2016 *Fleet Owner* Magazine named Gemini the nation's best private company carrier based on innovation, safety, and operations. For Brent and Frank, the highest achievement was 525 million miles on the road without an employee fatality.

While innovations in site selection and delivery of fuel helped expand the number of stores from coast to coast, horizontal expansion was not enough to achieve Tom Love's challenge of 16 percent annual growth and 16 percent annual net operating return. To reach the summit of that mountain, the Love's team needed to expand vertically, adding more profit centers at each location and finding new ways to gain market share.

The emergence of tire service as a major feature at Love's Travel Stops not only created new opportunities to attract truck drivers, but also posed challenges of recruiting and retaining skilled workers in a high risk business.

For the Love's team, it was a brave new world.

In many ways, the products and services feeding the growth of Love's stores were variations of products and services that had long served as the foundation of profitability. Gasoline, diesel, food, and merchandise were still critical to growth, but the line of products and services offered to truck drivers and the motoring public continued to grow with additional layers of profit centers without the need for additional real estate or employees.

This vertical expansion began with fuel and fuel supplements. As early as 2011, the Love's team experimented with bulk sales of propane from 1,000-gallon tanks. Customers for the additional product included pickups fueled by propane, recreational vehicles, and operators of light industrial equipment such as fork lifts and trenchers. An even larger market was developed through the sale of diesel exhaust fluid, referred to as DEF, that converted environmentally harmful carbon dioxide emissions to benign gasses. This emission control technology would be required on all new diesel engines made after 2017. From 2010, when the first DEF was offered at the pump alongside diesel, to 2017, Musket built thirteen DEF wholesale bulk racks across ten states where Gemini trucks loaded the product for distribution to stores.

An even more ambitious vertical market gamble was launched in 2010 when the Love's team installed the first compressed natural gas pumps at Travel Stops. At the time, when oil was soaring above $140 a barrel, the price differential between diesel and natural gas was wide enough to encourage the purchase of cars and trucks that could use the cleaner burning natural gas. By 2013, when Love's purchased fifty new Gemini trucks that burned natural gas, the CNG team led by Bill Cashmareck launched a plan to install fast-fill pumps in the Texas Triangle between Houston, Dallas, and San Antonio. At the time, CNG was $2 cheaper per gallon than diesel, and subsidies in natural gas-producing states like Texas and Oklahoma covered much of the upfront costs of installation. Then the market changed overnight.

In 2014, as horizontal drilling helped create a glut of crude, the price of oil plunged to less than $40 a barrel, which threw the price advantage back to diesel as the cost efficient fuel. To hedge their bets on natural gas as a fuel of the future, the Love's team looked for a niche that would keep them in the natural gas market. They found it in Wisconsin.

Jenny, Frank, and Gary Price met with workers in one of the many tire shops opened and expanded across the country.

In 2016 a public utility company was ordered to sell a private-market subsidiary called Trillium. For twenty years Chicago-based Trillium had designed, built, and operated a network of compressed natural gas fueling stations for Fortune 500 companies, trucking fleets, and public entities such as trash haulers, mass transit providers, and airports. At the time, Trillium was the second largest distributor of CNG in the country delivering more than 55 million equivalent gallons each year to their customers.

Even though they had always grown internally and avoided costly acquisitions, the Love's leadership team pounced on the opportunity to buy Trillium. "We had all the skill sets for buying and distributing CNG," said Greg Love, "so Trillium was simply an expansion of what we had been doing."

"The acquisition of Trillium CNG provided Love's with a great opportunity to leverage the very best of two companies," added Frank Love. "Trillium's deep expertise in the industry will allow Love's to serve new types of customers in new markets while expanding our reach to existing customers."

Viewed initially as a long-term hedge on CNG, the bolt-on acquisition quickly paid dividends. In 2017 the Trillium subsidiary signed a twenty-year deal with the Pennsylvania Department of Transportation to design, build, maintain, and supply twenty-nine CNG fueling facilities for more than 1,600 busses operated by transit agencies across the state. Seven of the locations were open to the general public. Bill Cashmareck summarized the harmony of the acquisition. "It is this ability to provide top-to-bottom CNG infrastructure that allows Love's to tap markets we've never had access to before," he said. While keeping their focus on the 40 percent of all busses in the country running on CNG, Bill and the Love's leadership team were keeping their options open for the day that CNG markets could expand again. In the meantime they were building expertise in CNG distribution and investing in people and places while experimenting with alternative services such as electric vehicle charging stations, solar panel installations, and hydrogen fueling.

A similar evolution opened the door to a growing business in truck tires. Love's had flirted with tire sales and service as early as 2008, when TA purchased Petro Truck Stops and forced the Michelin brand out of the Petro system. Michelin needed a company to do "emergency road service" for their customers and the Love's team was willing to experiment with a new enterprise. Starting with eight tire shops in Texas, most of which had one or two bays with storage for 200 tires, Love's grew to more than 130 tire centers with road service scattered along its system by 2014. The Love family thought they could do better.

In 2015 they asked Tom Edwards to delay retirement and oversee the expansion into the tire and light mechanical service sectors. "We realized we were just swimming in the shallow end of the pool with over-the-road emergency tire service," recalled Frank Love. "We needed to do a deep dive and take advantage of an opportunity." They started with larger shops, including air-conditioned waiting rooms and two to three bays for service. They expanded the choice of new tires beyond Michelin, including Bridgestone, Goodyear, Aeolus, BF Goodrich, and Yokohama, while elevating their brand of service to truckers twenty-four hours a day, 365 days a year. They experimented with light mechanical repairs at a few Travel Stops. The real leap forward, however, came where the rubber met the road.

As the Love's team had discovered with their own fleet of more than 500 Gemini trucks, a new virgin truck tire might cost $400 to $500, but each tire could be retreaded at a cost of $150, with up to three retreads per tire casing. In 2016 the Love's team announced plans to build four tire distribution centers in Dallas, Atlanta, Indianapolis, and Las Vegas, each with a retread plant, a large commercial warehouse to store new and retread tires, commercial sales office, conference facility, and dedicated fleet of trucks for tire distribution. Within one year the Atlanta plant was producing an average of 1,000 retreads a week with a work force of forty employees.

In late 2017, while growing their tire and service capabilities internally, the Love's team negotiated the purchase of Speedco, a highly regarded chain of fifty-two heavy duty truck lube centers scattered over thirty-seven states. With the acquisition came middle managers who knew how to deal with the fierce competition for skilled workers and safety hazards of the business. Aaron Aylworth, who had started the Love's Tire Centers ten years earlier, was named director of Speedco. "When we added Speedco to our mix," he said, "they made us the oil-change experts overnight. By adding us to them, they got a giant network six times their current size and an elaborate tire and light mechanical network. I think we enhanced each other well."

The acquisition also enhanced Love's reputation as the best "one-stop" shop in the trucking industry where time was becoming an increasingly valuable commodity. For big fleets, the opportunities for bundled services were attractive, while truck drivers earning money by the mile knew the quicker they could get fuel, tires, and service, along with showers, food, and equipment, the quicker they were back on the road with wheels rolling.

While Trillium and Speedco were bolt-on acquisitions that

The acquisition of Speedco was a major leap into vertical integration of services available to truck drivers who saw time saved as more miles on the road.

vertically expanded and enhanced existing enterprises, the Love's team eased their way into the unfamiliar world of hotel ownership. In some ways, hotels fit the Love's business model. Overnight accommodations were part of the traveling experience for both motorists and truckers, and many existing Love's Travel Stops had enough excess real estate on their existing footprint to explore this opportunity. The first hotel was opened in Pecos, Texas, in 2014, under third party management. By the end of 2017 there were seventeen Love's hotels operating under brands including Fairfield Inn, Choice Hotels, and Holiday Inn Express. In 2018, in yet another experiment, the Love's management team assumed day-to-day operations of this growing string of hotels.

As proven through the combination of new stores and bolt-on businesses such as hotels, Trillium, and Speedco, the Love's team was capable of doubling the size of the company in six years. Achieving the other goals set by Tom Love, such as exceeding 16 percent net operating return each year and maintaining the family culture at the heart of the company would require a similar commitment to team work and creativity.

It was time to strengthen the hub at the center of the rapidly turning wheel.

Hotels adjacent to Love's Travel Stops added another layer to services provided to customers and took advantage of real estate already owned.

Just as the Love's team had to balance growth with net operating return, they had to balance the ability of the headquarter staff to keep pace not only with an increasing number of stores and employees, but also with the increasing number of opportunities to use technology for improved efficiencies. Too little invested in infrastructure could leave the operational teams on the front lines without support, while too much invested in support staff, technology, and headquarters buildings could sap resources before they reached the front lines. Either could threaten the long term sustainability of Love's as a family owned business.

Carl Martincich was one of the senior managers struggling with that balancing act. Carl had joined the company as a twenty-one-year-old college graduate in 1982, and had risen through the ranks as a general manager, district manager, and division director. In 2014, when Tom Love threw down his challenge of doubling the size of the company by 2020, Carl was vice president of human resources with deep knowledge of every level of operations.

After making sure every employee got their paycheck on time, Carl's team had the primary duty of assisting all managers in the recruitment, hiring, review, and promotion of the work force. In January of 2014, Love's had a total staff of 11,000 people scattered from coast to coast. By January of 2018 the number of employees had exploded to more than 20,000. At the same time, the number of job applicants grew to 400,000 a year. Whether hiring or promoting, the task of keeping the leadership pipeline filled with talented, motivated men and women was critical to the overall success of Love's.

As the mountain of personnel data grew exponentially, Carl and his team approached the Love family with a suggestion. They could continue using their old technology systems and add more employees to the HR department, or they could invest millions of dollars in new software and improve the speed and efficiency of generating reports that would help managers make the right decisions. The family did not blink. The investment was made and the results were quickly evident. And while the size of the employee base had almost doubled, the HR staff remained the same size it had been in 2014.

Ginny Webb, chief information officer and vice president of technology, had a similar balancing act in terms of investment and performance during rapid growth. A native of Minnesota who graduated from the University of Oklahoma, Ginny and her team had three primary tasks within the company. One was maintaining core data infrastructure from work stations to data centers. Second was managing data. The third was support for projects. The Atlas system serves as a good example.

Carl Martincich, who started his career with Love's in 1982, was promoted to vice president of human resources with the task of filling the pipeline of talent with new recruits as the grand expansion accelerated.

Ginny Webb was recruited to lead the Love's team as chief information officer and vice president of technology as the company expanded both in terms of geography and complexity.

Late in 2017 Ginny's team rolled out Atlas, a new mobile-based workforce management system that helped field-level managers make better data-based decisions how to effectively deploy their teams, increase efficiencies, prioritize tasks, and provide reports on completion. At the same time, the system measured the amount of labor and other resources needed to accomplish tasks at the store level. Drew Graham, a division director encouraging his general managers to lean on the new data management tool, summarized its importance. "As Love's grows in store count," he wrote, "it becomes more and more important that we grow gracefully and deliberately."

As a result of this search for greater efficiencies and improved net returns on the front lines of customer service, the staff at the Oklahoma City headquarters grew. A good example of growth with good return on investments was Echo Media, a Love's division that unified graphic design throughout the stores and saved money in production. In 2015, operating from a 12,000-square-foot shop, the printing team produced billboard sheets at a cost of $357, while outsourcing the same product cost $958. Managers estimated that the company was saving about 60 percent in printing costs, with orders received by 2:00 in the afternoon shipped by the end of the day.

Judy, who co-chairs the Love's Giving Committee with Jenny, appeared at a grand opening celebration of the Catholic Charities new headquarters with Bob Ross, Governor Mary Fallin, and Patrick Raglow. Judy co-chaired the Catholic Charities Capital Campaign.

Jenny, reflecting the family's commitment to education, joined Talita DeNegri (principal), Archbishop Paul Coakley, Oklahoma City Mayor Mick Cornett, and Bob Ross at a ground breaking ceremony at Mount St. Mary's school.

Another internal operation that improved net profit and expanded product offerings was factoring, a service available to independent truckers who needed cash flow to operate efficiently. Love's, with healthy cash flow and abundant capital, purchased truckers' freight invoices at a discount. Truckers received cash up front to pay expenses and avoid the accounting paperwork of billing for services, while Love's made a profit for holding the freight invoices until the shippers paid. By January of 2018, under

Judy and the Love family made a major commitment to Positive Tomorrows, a school for homeless children in Oklahoma City.

Bill Lance, Judy Love, and Mike Turpen. As 2014 Allied Arts campaign co-chairs, Love ad Turpen had a record-breaking fundraising year, raising more than $3-million.

Tom Love, spreading the word about the future of Love's as a growth company that would remain family owned, at the University of San Diego, stating "All we have to do is reload and recalibrate."

the steady hand of the service's first manager Gary Morgan, the factoring operation employed a staff of almost 100 people.

In 2013, anticipating the growth in support staff and new operating divisions, the Love family purchased three buildings in Oklahoma City from Chesapeake Energy Corporation. At the time, they estimated that the additional 227,000 square feet of office space would support growth for the foreseeable future. In July of 2016, as growth more than doubled, Love's leased an empty department store building north of the main campus to centralize the call center functions under one roof with nearly 250 employees. The final addition to the headquarters campus puzzle was the acquisition of the old Hertz reservation center with approximately 120,000 square feet of space that eventually will be used to support future growth in the number of stores and services.

Yet another balancing act was to keep the family culture of Love's intact. The tools to accomplish that task included personal communication top to bottom, training, awards ceremonies, and a genuine concern for the well-being of all team members. Performance bonuses and career opportunities, combined with emergency assistance when needed and scholarships for education, showed a culture of caring for one another.

Caring for others had long been expressed through the generous philanthropy of the entire Love's workforce. In early 2018, for the nineteenth straight year, Love's team members raised money at each store for the Children's Miracle Network, a non-profit organization that serves 170 children's hospitals across North America. Love's store team members have raised more than $19 million that has helped treat millions of children.

Setting the pace of caring is the Love family. When a tornado destroyed much of Moore, Oklahoma, the family donated $3 million to ease the personal suffering. When flooding hit Houston, the family donated $1million to the relief effort. Judy Love, the First Lady of Love's, serves as chairperson of the Love's charitable giving committee. The list of organizations receiving funds from Love's is long and distinguished . When interviewed for a magazine article in early 2018, Judy was serving as co-chair for a fund raising effort to build a new school for homeless children in Oklahoma City called Positive Tomorrows. "Hearing about the thousands of children who have no homes, not enough food, often no shoes, and they are falling behind in school or not attending regularly...I knew we could help," she said.

And Love's did help.

Love's Shares celebration at
LEAD Conference, giving away
$3.4-million to field employees.

Jenny Love Meyer at
CMN Dance Marathon..

Aubrey McClendon Tribute with chairs
Judy Love, Mike Turpen, and Bob Ross.

In April of 2018, while the expansion was still taking form, Tom and Frank Love spoke before a prominent business roundtable organization in Oklahoma City. Their topic was Love's Travel Stops and Country Stores.

Frank described the company after four years in the fast lane of expansion: 458 locations in 41 states, 723 restaurants, 335 Tire Care Centers, 52 Speedco Centers, 17 hotels, and more than 20,000 employees. He talked about the acquisition of Trillium, the nation's second largest player in municipal CNG markets, the launch of the truck tire business, including retread manufacturing, and the acquisition of Speedco, including the expansion into light mechanical truck service.

Tom, taking the microphone, told the story of the challenge he delivered to his family and staff in January of 2014. "Many of them thought it was a joke," he remembered. "I knew it would be life changing for everyone at Love's." He talked about the leadership team and his confidence in their unified support. He talked about the competition, including Warren Buffett's plans to buy a majority stake in Pilot/Flying J. But instead of describing that purchase as a negative threat, Tom turned it into a positive promise for the future of Love's. "Warren is rhapsodical about the future of America," he said, "and so am I."

As if looking into the future, he added, "All we have to do is recalibrate and reload."

Tom and Judy Love at the i2E Love's Cup Reception.

The Tom Love Innovation Hub Ribbon Cutting Ceremony at the University of Oklahoma.

TOP BANANA AWARDS

Tom Love and the Sizzle Sisters—Wanda Meador, Carol Willett, Jennifer Hast, Elena Knodel, DeNease Vinyard, and Linda Campbell.

In 1985, Tom Love began personally writing a script for a skit to be performed by employees during the annual Christmas luncheon where the Top Banana Award recipient also would be announced . The Top Banana Award is presented to a Love's employee who exemplifies leadership, commitment, and team spirit.

In Tom's typical showman style he strategically includes the employee who would be named Top Banana as a member of the cast. After announcing the winner of the award the Sizzle Sisters—a group of employees who sing at the annual event—break into song with lyrics including "you, you are the Top Banana—the one chosen over all the rest."

Although he has turned the skit production over to the public relations department, Tom is still on stage to announce the Top Banana and is an active participant in the festivities surrounding the event.

On the following pages are the winners of the Top Banana Award, created and nurtured by Tom to recognize leadership and team spirit. Ron Knight, the 1989 recipient, is not pictured.

1985   Larry Dillard

1986   Jerry Smith

1987   Wilma Baird

1987   Harold Wells

1988   Larry Sullivan

1990   Stella Scott

1991   Paula Downing

1992   Vern Meng

1993   Susan Hinckley

1994   Reta Harlin, Reba Baker

1995   Mike Herman

1996   Dave Gibbon

1997   Jana Sanders

1998   Grant Wilson

1999   Carl Martincich

2000   Terry Ross

2001   Len Chadwick

2002, 2005   Tom Squires

2003   Sherry Blagg

2004   DeNease Vinyard

2006   Mark Romig

2007   Linda Tillinghast

2008   Brent Bergevin

2009   Dion Crider

2010   Doug Stussi

2011   Rick Shuffield

2012   Dan Jensen

2013   Carol Willet

2014   Roger Ahuja

2015   Tracey Patterson and Betsy Baustert

2016   Robin Howard and
        Barbara Young

2017 Kelly Mason and Billy Clifton

STORE OPENINGS 2015

"It has taken us fifty years to build this company to its current size. Let's double it by 2020."

TOM LOVE, 2014

533 WILLIAMS, AZ

537 CUMBERLAND, MD

538 LODI, CA

577 SHORTER, AL

583 NEW BADEN, IL

585 NEOSHO, MO

589 LUBBOCK, TX

594 BIDWELL, OH

600 INGALLS, IN

601 KNIGHTSTOWN, IN

602 BOX ELDER, SD

603 JACKSONVILLE, FL

604 GUTHRIE, OK

607 JONESBORO, AR

608 MCPHERSON, KS

614 ALBUQUERQUE, NM

617 HUNGERFORD, TX

618 SADIEVILLE, KY

619 POPLARVILLE, MS

621 BEVIER, MO

622 MENOMONIE, WI

624 PRICHARD, AL

628 ITALY, TX

2015,(CONT.)

STORE OPENINGS 2016

648 VALLIANT, OK

93 GARDEN CITY, KS.JPG

115 BUENA VISTA, CO

654 UNION CITY, OK

116 MEADE, KS

117 CRESCENT, OK

BAIRD, TX

595 GULFPORT, MISS

606 SOUTH HOLLAND, IL

WOODBURN, IN

611 CANAAN, NY

612 BRIDGETON, MO

613 MEADOWVIEW, VA

616 HARRISONVILLE, MO

620 HAWTHORNE, FL

623 MIDLAND, TX

625 SIDNEY, NE

626 DUMAS, TX

627 DAVENPORT, FL

629 WHITE HOUSE, TN

630 ENID, OK

631 VALLEY, NE

632 LIBERAL, KS

633 PLYMOUTH, IN

636 NOWATA, OK

637 DEKORRA, WIS

638 TEXHOMA, OK

639 LAKE, MISS

641 DYERSBURG, TN

643 SIKESTON MO

644 BURLINGTON, CO

647 BELLEVILLE, KS

650 BOARDAMN, OR

651 VAN, TX

653 EADS, CO

655 SCOTT CITY, KS

656 HOLCOMB, KS

657 CAYCE, SC

658 WATTS, OK

659 TOLLESON, AZ

662 QUANAH, TX WITH TOM LOVE

662 QUANAH, TX

663 PORT BARRE, LA

664 TERRE HAUTE, IN

669 NEW LONDON, MISSOURI

670 FLOYD, IOWA

671 BLYTHEVILLE, AR

673 DOMINO, TX

675 OKMULGEE, OK

680 NORFOLK, NE

684 ELLSWORTH, IOWA

687 SOUTH JACKSONVILLE, IL

STORE OPENINGS 2017

605 SPRINGFIELD, OH

640 WILSON-SHEBOYGAN, WI

642 HEREFORD, TX

649 BRUSH, CO

661 PINE BLUFF, AR

665 ANGLETON, TX

667 MEBANE, NC

672 SINTON, TX

676 SYRACUSE, NE

677 WEST POINT, MS

678 PARIS, TX

679 HARDIN, MT

681 PROSSER, WA

682 HAGERSTOWN, MD

683 MOORE HAVEN, FL

685 KNOXVILLE, IL

686 BRIGHAM CITY, UT

688 GREENUP, IL

690 CIRCLEVILLE, OH

691 ELY, NV

692 CHANUTE, KS

693 UPPER SANDUSKY, OH

694 EASTVIEW, TN

695 CUNNINGHAM, KS

696 BEAUMONT, TX

697 NEWTON, NC

698 MACON, GA

699 MAGEE, MS

2017,(CONT.)

703 SOUTH HUTCHINSON, KS

705 TALLEYSVILLE, VA

708 BUSHNELL, FL

711 BELLVILLE, OH

712 NEWCASTLE, OK

713 BRIDGEPORT, TX

718 HOPE HULL, AL

719 TROY, TX

STORE OPENINGS 2018

118 WYNEWOOD, OK

257 MILAN, NM

497 STATESVILLE, NC

609 DENTON, TX

635 ALMA, AK

701 CAPAC, MI

702 WATERLOO, IA

704 MILLS COUNTY, IA

709 LUFKIN, TX

716 ELIZABETHTOWN, KY

717 PRINCE GEORGE, VA

720 BOYCE, LA

2018,(CONT.)

721 ALMA, TEXAS

724 ELLISVILLE FL

725 HANSON, KY

726 BALEN, NM

728 MILLERSBURG, OR

732 ABILENE, KS

733 LAS VEGAS, NM

734 RANDLETT, OK

739 DONNA, TX

1972-2018 LOVE'S STORES LIST

JANUARY 1, 1972: WATONGA, OK
JULY 1, 1972: FAIRVIEW, OK
OCTOBER 1, 1972: BUFFALO, OK
MARCH 13, 1973: SYRACUSE, KS
JUNE 5, 1973: LAMAR, CO
JUNE 14, 1973: SPRINGFIELD, CO
JULY 2, 1973: GUYMON, OK
APRIL 3, 1974: BEAVER, OK
MAY 23, 1974: CLAYTON, NM
SEPTEMBER 17, 1974: LAMAR, CO
OCTOBER 10, 1974: PURCELL, OK
DECEMBER 15, 1974: LIBERAL, KS
AUGUST 22, 1975: LAJUNTA, CO
DECEMBER 20, 1975: MONTE VISTA, CO
MARCH 4, 1976: GUNNISON, CO
MARCH 16, 1976: KINGFISHER, OK
SEPTEMBER 19, 1976: ALTUS, OK
DECEMBER 19, 1976: ELK CITY, OK
FEBRUARY 14, 1977: MANGUM, OK
APRIL 3, 1977: HOLLIS, OK
MAY 28, 1977: WOODWARD, OK
JULY 7, 1977: PRATT, KS
AUGUST 19, 1977: ALVA, OK
MAY 6, 1978: GREAT BEND, KS
JUNE 14, 1978: SHAWNEE, OK
JUNE 21, 1978: TECUMSEH, OK
JUNE 24, 1978: DODGE CITY, KS
JULY 18, 1978: DODGE CITY, KS
AUGUST 4, 1978: ADA, OK
SEPTEMBER 7, 1978: HENNESSEY, OK
OCTOBER 12, 1978: PAULS VALLEY, OK
OCTOBER 18, 1978: WOODWARD, OK
NOVEMBER 13, 1978: ARDMORE, OK
DECEMBER 7, 1978: COLBY, KS
DECEMBER 9, 1978: MARLOW, OK
DECEMBER 16, 1978: HAYS, KS
JANUARY 25, 1979: COMANCHE, OK
FEBRUARY 28, 1979: PHILLIPSBURG, KS
APRIL 9, 1979: HENRYETTA, OK
APRIL 22, 1979: HOOKER, OK
APRIL 28, 1979: NORTON, KS
OCTOBER 12, 1979: MARLOW, OK
MARCH 14, 1980: DURANT, OK
APRIL 29, 1980: LINDSAY, OK
MAY 9, 1980: MIAMI, OK
MAY 24, 1980: DURANT, OK
JUNE 26, 1980: TAHLEQUAH, OK
DECEMBER 21, 1980: MADILL, OK
JANUARY 11, 1981: ADA, OK
FEBRUARY 18, 1981: CHICKASHA, OK
MARCH 6, 1981: BROKEN BOW, OK
MARCH 26, 1981: GUTHRIE, OK
APRIL 17, 1981: YUKON, OK
DECEMBER 9, 1981: ARKANSAS CITY, KS
JULY 19, 1982: ELK CITY, OK
SEPTEMBER 4, 1982: OKLAHOMA CITY, OK
SEPTEMBER 30, 1982: DUNCAN, OK
DECEMBER 19, 1982: EDMOND, OK
FEBRUARY 9, 1983: CHICKASHA, OK
APRIL 29, 1983: EL RENO, OK
MARCH 22, 1984: OKLAHOMA CITY, OK
MAY 10, 1984: ALBUQUERQUE, NM
OCTOBER 26, 1985: DENTON, TX
OCTOBER 14, 1986: EL PASO, TX
NOVEMBER 15, 1986: GALLUP, NM
APRIL 21, 1988: OKLAHOMA CITY, OK
SEPTEMBER 8, 1988: SEMINOLE, OK
FEBRUARY 25, 1989: CLINTON, OK
APRIL 7, 1989: CLAUDE, TX
MAY 5, 1989: AMARILLO, TX
MAY 22, 1989: ERICK, OK
SEPTEMBER 15, 1989: MCLOUD, OK
FEBRUARY 15, 1990: VAN HORN, TX
MAY 11, 1990: NORMAN, OK
JUNE 25, 1990: MILAN, NM
AUGUST 10, 1990: AMARILLO, TX

AUGUST 24, 1990: LAS CRUCES, NM
FEBRUARY 22, 1991: LULING, TX
MAY 10, 1991: LAWTON, OK
OCTOBER 11, 1991: TUCUMCARI, NM
APRIL 28, 1994: MORRILTON, AR
JUNE 5, 1994: ARDMORE, OK
NOVEMBER 12, 1994: ATOKA, OK
DECEMBER 14, 1994: WICHITA FALLS, TX
MAY 20, 1995: RANGER, TX
JUNE 19, 1995: OZARK, AR
DECEMBER 2, 1995: N. LITTLE ROCK, AR
MARCH 15, 1996: WEATHERFORD, TX
APRIL 13, 1996: OKEMAH, OK
MAY 20, 1996: LORDSBURG, NM
SEPTEMBER 22, 1996: MT. VERNON, TX
FEBRUARY 16, 1997: BUCKEYE, AZ
MAY 24, 1997: FT. WORTH, TX
OCTOBER 16, 1997: PALESTINE, AR
NOVEMBER 3, 1997: QUARTZSITE, AZ
NOVEMBER 22, 1997: JOSEPH CITY, AZ
SEPTEMBER 23, 1998: GILA BEND, AZ
NOVEMBER 9, 1998: CHOUTEAU, OK
DECEMBER 3, 1998: LUFKIN, TX
FEBRUARY 9, 1999: SANTA ROSA, NM
FEBRUARY 22, 1999: VAN, TX
APRIL 14, 1999: ELOY, AZ
JULY 16, 1999: PRESCOTT, AR
SEPTEMBER 21, 1999: PORT ALLEN, LA
SEPTEMBER 28, 1999: JACKSON, TN
OCTOBER 1, 1999: GUTHRIE, OK
OCTOBER 19, 1999: IOWA, LA
DECEMBER 10, 1999: EDNA, TX
FEBRUARY 8, 2000: FAIRFIELD, TX
MARCH 2, 2000: DALLAS, TX
MAY 12, 2000: EUFAULA, OK
MAY 19, 2000: AMARILLO, TX
AUGUST 22, 2000: VON ORMY, TX
SEPTEMBER 20, 2000: CANTON, MS
OCTOBER 17, 2000: JOPLIN, MO
OCTOBER 31, 2000: LOXLEY, AL
DECEMBER 19, 2000: COACHELLA, CA
DECEMBER 19, 2000: RICHMOND, IN
JUNE 12, 2001: WALLER, TX
JULY 17, 2001: ROCKWALL, TX
AUGUST 7, 2001: ANNA, TX
AUGUST 28, 2001: RIPON, CA
AUGUST 31, 2001: TONKAWA, OK
SEPTEMBER 26, 2001: ENCINAL/LAREDO, TX
OCTOBER 30, 2001: SHEPHERDSVILLE, KY
NOVEMBER 21, 2001: ZANESVILLE, OH
DECEMBER 13, 2001: MAX MEADOWS, VA
APRIL 3, 2002: HILLSBORO, TX
JUNE 8, 2002: RICHMOND, LA
JULY 1, 2002: KINGMAN, AZ
AUGUST 20, 2002: MIDLOTHIAN, TX
NOVEMBER 12, 2002: CHEYENNE, WY
DECEMBER 19, 2002: LOST HILLS, CA
MARCH 6, 2003: ST. JOSEPH, MO
MARCH 28, 2003: DANDRIDGE, TN
APRIL 17, 2003: GREENWOOD, LA
APRIL 24, 2003: WILLIAMSVILLE, IL
MAY 8, 2003: AUBURNDALE, FL
MAY 22, 2003: JACKSON, GA
JULY 21, 2003: TOM'S BROOK, VA
AUGUST 7, 2003: EDINBURG, TX
AUGUST 21, 2003: FERNLEY, NV
OCTOBER 9, 2003: MARION, NC
NOVEMBER 6, 2003: RICHMOND, KY
NOVEMBER 13, 2003: AURORA, NE
DECEMBER 4, 2003: WAMSUTTER, WY
MARCH 19, 2004: ROSEBURG, OR
APRIL 1, 2004: WACO, GA
MAY 20, 2004: HOUSTON, TX
MAY 28, 2004: MATTHEWS, MO
JULY 8, 2004: CHRISTIANA, TN
AUGUST 19, 2004: INA, IL

AUGUST 26, 2004: KATY, TX
OCTOBER 21, 2004: DUBLIN, GA
NOVEMBER 4, 2004: CLOVIS, NM
NOVEMBER 18, 2004: PITTSBORO, IN
DECEMBER 14, 2004: SKIPPERS, VA
DECEMBER 16, 2004: CORBIN, KY
JANUARY 20, 2005: TIFTON, GA
FEBRUARY 3, 2005: MARION, IN
FEBRUARY 10, 2005: ROSCOE, IL
FEBRUARY 24, 2005: ORANGEBURG, SC
JULY 21, 2005: KINGSVILLE, TX
AUGUST 4, 2005: CHANDLER, AZ
SEPTEMBER 1, 2005: BAXTER, TN
SEPTEMBER 29, 2005: MIFFLINVILLE, PA
NOVEMBER 3, 2005: HEYBURN, ID
NOVEMBER 17, 2005: MARSHALL, MI
JANUARY 5, 2006: FORT MILL, SC
JANUARY 12, 2006: HUTCHINS, TX
JANUARY 19, 2006: CEDAR CITY, UT
JANUARY 26, 2006: TOOMSUBA, MS
MARCH 16, 2006: RICHMOND HILL, GA
MARCH 16, 2006: ODESSA, TX
JULY 27, 2006: ROLLA, MO
AUGUST 3, 2006: ORMOND BEACH, FL
AUGUST 10, 2006: MEMPHIS, IN
SEPTEMBER 14, 2006: COLUMBIA, TN
SEPTEMBER 21, 2006: CALVERT CITY, KY
SEPTEMBER 28, 2006: JEFFERSONVILLE, OH
OCTOBER 26, 2006: THOMSON, GA
DECEMBER 7, 2006: MINDEN, LA
DECEMBER 14, 2006: ALBERT LEA, MN
DECEMBER 14, 2006: UTICA, IL
JANUARY 4, 2007: BURBANK, OH
JANUARY 4, 2007: N BALTIMORE, OH
MARCH 22, 2007: YUMA, AZ
MAY 17, 2007: MEMPHIS, TN
AUGUST 16, 2007: VINTON, LA
AUGUST 23, 2007: BOONVILLE, MO
AUGUST 29, 2007: HORSE CAVE, KY
AUGUST 30, 2007: FOUNTAIN, CO
SEPTEMBER 20, 2007: CLANTON, AL
NOVEMBER 8, 2007: CHARLESTON, TN
NOVEMBER 15, 2007: TOMAH, WI
NOVEMBER 15, 2007: DILLON, SC
DECEMBER 13, 2007: JONESTOWN, PA
DECEMBER 20, 2007: LE ROY, IL
JANUARY 3, 2008: HINTON, OK
JANUARY 17, 2008: NEWTON, IA
JANUARY 31, 2008: HUDSON, CO
MARCH 20, 2008: COLBERT, OK
MARCH 27, 2008: HOGANSVILLE, GA
APRIL 3, 2008: LEE, FL
MAY 22, 2008: HUBBARD, OH
MAY 29, 2008: FALKVILLE, AL
JUNE 25, 2008: WELLS, NV
JULY 24, 2008: SPARTA, KY
AUGUST 13, 2008: OKLAHOMA CITY, OK
NOVEMBER 13, 2008: RIPLEY, WV
NOVEMBER 20, 2008: HAMBURG, PA
DECEMBER 4, 2008: ONTARIO, OR
APRIL 9, 2009: LAKE HAVASU, AZ
MAY 7, 2009: MCCOMB, MS
MAY 14, 2009: CLEVELAND, TX
JUNE 4, 2009: BARSTOW, CA
AUGUST 27, 2009: BLACKSBURG, SC
SEPTEMBER 17, 2009: NEWBERRY, SC
NOVEMBER 12, 2009: GREENVILLE, IL
DECEMBER 3, 2009: NORTH PLATTE, NE
DECEMBER 3, 2009: ST. PAUL, IN
JANUARY 14, 2010: STEELE, AL
JANUARY 21, 2010: TULARE, CA
FEBRUARY 18, 2010: LAMBSBURG, VA
MARCH 11, 2010: N. LAS VEGAS, NV
APRIL 1, 2010: MEMPHIS, TX
APRIL 22, 2010: BOISE CITY, OK
MAY 20, 2010: WADDY, KY
JUNE 10, 2010: BATESVILLE, MS
JUNE 10, 2010: TUPELO, MS
JUNE 17, 2010: EVERGREEN, AL
JULY 1, 2010: CORNING, CA
JULY 1, 2010: DES MOINES, IA

JULY 1, 2010: GARY, IN
JULY 1, 2010: OAK CREEK, WI
JULY 1, 2010: TACOMA, WA
JULY 1, 2010: TROUTDALE, OR
JULY 2, 2010: SIOUX FALLS, SD
JULY 6, 2010: BILOXI, MS
JULY 6, 2010: BINGHAMTON, NY
JULY 6, 2010: WEST MEMPHIS, AR
JULY 6, 2010: WHITELAND, IN
JULY 7, 2010: BORDENTOWN, NJ
JULY 7, 2010: FORT PIERCE, FL
JULY 7, 2010: GRAYSON, KY
JULY 7, 2010: FLOWOOD, MS
JULY 7, 2010: SALT LAKE CITY, UT
JULY 8, 2010: BAYTOWN, TX
JULY 8, 2010: BRUNSWICK, GA
JULY 8, 2010: CARLISLE, PA
JULY 8, 2010: ELLENSBURG, WA
JULY 8, 2010: HAUBSTADT, IN
JULY 9, 2010: DUNN, NC
JULY 9, 2010: HOUSTON, TX
JULY 9, 2010: NASHVILLE, TN
JULY 9, 2010: RUTHER GLEN, VA
JULY 9, 2010: SANTA NELLA, CA
JULY 22, 2010: FAIR PLAY, SC
AUGUST 12, 2010: THREE RIVERS, TX
AUGUST 20, 2010: TEHACHAPI, CA
AUGUST 26, 2010: MCCALLA, AL
SEPTEMBER 23, 2010: CONNEAUT, OH
NOVEMBER 18, 2010: FARGO, ND
FEBRUARY 9, 2011: ELLIS, KS
MARCH 31, 2011: PUEBLO, CO
APRIL 28, 2011: HEARNE, TX
MAY 4, 2011: BENSON, AZ
MAY 5, 2011: DICKSON, TN
MAY 12, 2011: CARTERSVILLE, GA
JUNE 9, 2011: OCALA, FL
JUNE 30, 2011: RHOME, TX
AUGUST 25, 2011: PAULS VALLEY, OK
SEPTEMBER 8, 2011: POST FALLS, ID
SEPTEMBER 15, 2011: BENNETT, CO
SEPTEMBER 22, 2011: NAPAVINE, WA
SEPTEMBER 29, 2011: COTTONDALE, FL
OCTOBER 6, 2011: DEMOTTE, IN
OCTOBER 13, 2011: BENSON, AZ
OCTOBER 20, 2011: PERRYSBURG, OH
OCTOBER 27, 2011: OTTAWA, KS
NOVEMBER 10, 2011: STRAFFORD, MO
NOVEMBER 17, 2011: MOORESVILLE (BELLEVILLE), IN
DECEMBER 1, 2011: WHITESTOWN, IN
DECEMBER 8, 2011: KANKAKEE, IL
DECEMBER 15, 2011: DWIGHT, IL
DECEMBER 15, 2011: LITTLE ROCK, AR
FEBRUARY 16, 2012: SEGUIN, TX
MARCH 29, 2012: COMFORT, TX
MAY 3, 2012: JASPER, AL
MAY 31, 2012: ANTHONY, TX
AUGUST 16, 2012: WILLIS, TX
AUGUST 23, 2012: SIOUX CITY, IA
AUGUST 30, 2012: JASPER, FL
SEPTEMBER 13, 2012: LACROSSE, VA
NOVEMBER 15, 2012: TEXARKANA, TX
NOVEMBER 15, 2012: WILLISTON, ND
DECEMBER 13, 2012: DAVENPORT, IA
DECEMBER 13, 2012: IDAHO FALLS, ID
FEBRUARY 7, 2013: WEBBERS FALLS, OK
FEBRUARY 14, 2013: NATALIA, TX
MARCH 7, 2013: SWEETWATER, TX
APRIL 25, 2013: WEIMAR, TX
JUNE 18, 2013: DEER PARK, TX
JUNE 27, 2013: LENOIR CITY, TN
OCTOBER 17, 2013: EAGLEVILLE, MO
OCTOBER 24, 2013: NICKAJACK LAKE, TN
OCTOBER 31, 2013: RITZVILLE, WA
NOVEMBER 21, 2013: BLOOMSDALE, MO
DECEMBER 5, 2013: DAYTON, OH
DECEMBER 12, 2013: PECOS, TX
DECEMBER 12, 2013: ST. LOUIS, MO
DECEMBER 12, 2013: LEXINGTON, SC
JANUARY 23, 2014: MOODY, AL
JANUARY 30, 2014: SPRINGVILLE, UT

FEBRUARY 13, 2014: DUSON, LA
MARCH 13, 2014: ANDREWS, TX
APRIL 3, 2014: SALISBURY, NC
APRIL 10, 2014: OGLESBY, IL
MAY 8, 2014: FT. PIERCE, FL
MAY 15, 2014: OKC, OK (CHOCTAW RD.)
JUNE 5, 2014: GRAND JUNCTION, CO
JUNE 5, 2014: DODGE CITY, KS
JULY 24, 2014: SEARCY, AR
AUGUST 14, 2014: SHELBY, IA
AUGUST 14, 2014: FORT MYERS, FL
AUGUST 21, 2014: FRANKLIN, VA
AUGUST 21, 2014: ANGOLA, IN
AUGUST 21, 2014: INDIANOLA, MS
AUGUST 28, 2014: MOSSY HEAD, FL
AUGUST 28, 2014: FT. STOCKTON, TX
OCTOBER 2, 2014: OZARK, AL
OCTOBER 30, 2014: MUSCLE SHOALS, AL
NOVEMBER 13, 2014: COLUMBUS, MS
NOVEMBER 20, 2014: SALINA, UT
NOVEMBER 20, 2014: FOND DU LAC, WI
DECEMBER 18, 2014: HAMEL, IL
DECEMBER 18, 2014: LONDONDERRY TOWNSHIP, PA
FEBRUARY 12, 2015: INGALLS, IN
FEBRUARY 19, 2015: BIDWELL, OH
MARCH 19, 2015: BOX ELDER, SD
APRIL 9, 2015: WILLIAMS, AZ
APRIL 16, 2015: LODI, CA
APRIL 23, 2015: NEOSHO, MO
APRIL 30, 2015: MCPHERSON, KS
MAY 7, 2015: WOODBURN, IN
MAY 7, 2015: BAIRD, TX
MAY 21, 2015: JACKSONVILLE, FL
JUNE 4, 2015: NEW BADEN, IL
JUNE 11, 2015: POPLARVILLE, MS
JUNE 25, 2015: SHORTER, AL
JULY 2, 2015: JONESBORO, AR
JULY 2, 2015: BEVIER, MO
JULY 23, 2015: KNIGHTSTOWN, IN
SEPTEMBER 3, 2015: LUBBOCK, TX
OCTOBER 1, 2015: HUNGERFORD, TX
OCTOBER 22, 2015: PRICHARD, AL
OCTOBER 29, 2015: ITALY, TX
NOVEMBER 19, 2015: CUMBERLAND, MD
NOVEMBER 19, 2015: MENOMONIE, WI
NOVEMBER 21, 2015: ALBUQUERQUE, NM
DECEMBER 2, 2015: VALLIANT, OK
DECEMBER 10, 2015: GUTHRIE, OK
DECEMBER 10, 2015: SADIEVILLE, KY
DECEMBER 17, 2015: UNION CITY, OK
JANUARY 14, 2016: TEXHOMA, OK
JANUARY 21, 2016: VALLEY, NE
JANUARY 28, 2016: HOLCOMB, KS
FEBRUARY 4, 2016: GARDEN CITY, KS
MARCH 10, 2016: BURLINGTON, CO
MARCH 10, 2016: PLYMOUTH, IN
MARCH 10, 2016: NOWATA, OK
MARCH 17, 2016: MIDLAND, TX
MARCH 17, 2016: SIKESTON, MO
MARCH 17, 2016: BUENA VISTA, CO
MARCH 17, 2016: SCOTT CITY, KS
MARCH 31, 2016: CANAAN, NY
APRIL 21, 2016: DAVENPORT, FL
MAY 19, 2016: DUMAS, TX
MAY 19, 2016: SIDNEY, NE
JUNE 9, 2016: BOARDMAN, OR
JUNE 16, 2016: MEADOWVIEW, VA
JUNE 16, 2016: TOLLESON, AZ
JUNE 23, 2016: ENID, OK
JUNE 30, 2016: BELLEVILLE, KS
JUNE 30, 2016: LIBERAL, KS
JULY 21, 2016: VAN, TX
JULY 28, 2016: BRIDGETON, MO
JULY 28, 2016: HARRISONVILLE, MO
JULY 28, 2016: QUANAH, TX
AUGUST 4, 2016: BLYTHEVILLE, AR
AUGUST 4, 2016: HAWTHORNE, FL
AUGUST 11, 2016: DYERSBURG, TN
SEPTEMBER 15, 2016: LAKE, MS
SEPTEMBER 15, 2016: OKMULGEE, OK
SEPTEMBER 15, 2016: MEADE, KS

SEPTEMBER 29, 2016: TERRE HAUTE, IN
OCTOBER 6, 2016: PORT BARRE, LA
OCTOBER 20, 2016: GULFPORT, MS
OCTOBER 27, 2016: WEST SILOAM SPRINGS, OK
NOVEMBER 3, 2016: EADS, OK
NOVEMBER 10, 2016: SOUTH HOLLAND, IL
NOVEMBER 17, 2016: DOMINO, TX
NOVEMBER 17, 2016: WHITE HOUSE, TN
DECEMBER 1, 2016: DEKORRA, WI
DECEMBER 1, 2016: CRESCENT, OK
DECEMBER 8, 2016: FLOYD, IA
DECEMBER 15, 2016: NEW LONDON, MO
DECEMBER 15, 2016: ELLSWORTH, IA
DECEMBER 15, 2016: NORFOLK, NE
DECEMBER 15, 2016: SO. JACKSONVILLE, IL
DECEMBER 15, 2016: CAYCE, SC
JANUARY 12, 2017: ANGLETON, TX
JANUARY 12, 2017: SYRACUSE, NE
JANUARY 26, 2017: SPRINGFIELD, OH
JANUARY 26, 2017: HEREFORD, TX
JANUARY 26, 2017: CUNNINGHAM, KS
FEBRUARY 9, 2017: CHANUTE, KS
FEBRUARY 16, 2017: KNOXVILLE, IL
FEBRUARY 23, 2017: GREENUP, IL
FEBRUARY 23, 2017: BRIGHAM CITY, UT
MARCH 9, 2017: HAGERSTOWN, MD
MARCH 23, 2017: MOORE HAVEN, FL
APRIL 27, 2017: UPPER SANDUSKY, OH
APRIL 27, 2017: MACON, GA
MAY 11, 2017: SINTON, TX
MAY 18, 2017: SOUTH HUTCHINSON, KS
MAY 25, 2017: PROSSER, WA
MAY 25, 2017: PARIS, TX
JUNE 8, 2017: HARDIN, MT
JUNE 15, 2017: WILSON TOWNSHIP, WI
JUNE 29, 2017: ELY, NV
JULY 13, 2017: WEST POINT, MS
JULY 13, 2017: CIRCLEVILLE, OH
JULY 20, 2017: MAGEE, MS
AUGUST 3, 2017: MEBANE, NC
AUGUST 24, 2017: NEWTON, NC
AUGUST 24, 2017: BEAUMONT, TX
SEPTEMBER 21, 2017: TALLEYSVILLE, VA
OCTOBER 19, 2017: NEWCASTLE, OK
DECEMBER 7, 2017: BRIDGEPORT, TX
DECEMBER 7, 2017: EASTVIEW, TN
DECEMBER 7, 2017: PINE BLUFF, AR
DECEMBER 14, 2017: BUSHNELL, FL
DECEMBER 14, 2017: HOPE HULL, AL
DECEMBER 14, 2017: BELLVILLE, OH
DECEMBER 14, 2017: BRUSH, CO
DECEMBER 18, 2017: TROY, TX
JANUARY 18, 2018: ALMA, AR
FEBRUARY 1, 2018: MILLS COUNTY, IA
FEBRUARY 1, 2018: ALMA, TX
FEBRUARY 8, 2018: WATERLOO, IA
FEBRUARY 22, 2018: PRINCE GEORGE, VA
MARCH 1, 2018: WYNNEWOOD, OK
MARCH 9, 2018: DENTON, TX
MARCH 15, 2018: ELIZABETHTOWN, KY
MARCH 22, 2018: CAPAC, MI
MAY 3, 2018: RANDLETT, OK
MAY 3, 2018: BELEN, NM
MAY 17, 2018: BOYCE, LA
MAY 24, 2018: HANSON, KY
MAY 24, 2018: LUFKIN, TX
JUNE 7, 2018: STATESVILLE, NC
JUNE 7, 2018: MILAN (R&R), NM
JUNE 7, 2018: ELLISVILLE, FL
JUNE 28, 2018: LAS VEGAS, NM
JULY 26, 2018: ABILENE, KS
AUGUST 9, 2018: DONNA, TX
AUGUST 16, 2018: MILLERSBURG, OR
SEPTEMBER 6, 2018: BERTHOUND, CO
SEPTEMBER 10, 2018: TIPTON, IN
SEPTEMBER 13, 2018: BASTIAN, VA
SEPTEMBER 13, 2018: FRENCHTOWN, MI
SEPTEMBER 13, 2018: LARAMIE, WY

LOVE'S FAMILY GALLERY

The Love family through the years.

Left to right, back row: Laura, Greg, Jenny; front row Judy, Tom, Frank.

Judy and Tom Love "love" spending time with their grandchildren.

Tom with his children and grandchildren.

Judy and Tom with grandchildren on annual Crested Butte ski trip.

Greg and Judy, holding new grandson Thomas.

Tom and Judy with their first grandchild Francie.

Tom holding new granddaughter Aly, with grandchildren Thomas, David, and Francie.

Gordon Dinsmore

One of the many trips to the
Oklahoma State Fair with the
grandchildren.

Standing, from left, Tom, his mother
Margaret Vessels Love, Thomas,
and Judy. Seated, Caroline, Francie,
Claire, Liza, and David.

The Love's Corporate Rowing Team won gold medals in the Novice Category of the fall 2013 River Regatta. Pictured with honorary captain Judy Love are, from left, front row, Kris Rogers and Kyla Turner, and, back row, Jennifer Clair, Robert Hirschman, Coach Jake Lamb, Joe Stallings, Ashley Young, Chris Gray, and Brent Hart.

The University of San Diego (USD) wins the 1985 Crew Classic Championship. Third from left is Laura Love who rowed for USD and went on to coach novice rowing upon graduation.

Tom, Frank, and David relaxing
after a day of fishing.

Frank, Tom, and Greg on a "guy's" fishing trip.

Frank and Malia Love, Brenda McDaniel, and Judy cheering
on the Oklahoma City Thunder's Russell Westbrook.

Tom with his daughters, Laura, left, and Jenny, right, with granddaughters, from left, Caroline, Liza, Claire, and Aly.

Judy celebrating her 50th wedding anniversary with granddaughters, back row from left, Claire, Caroline, Judy, Liza, and Francie and front row, Emma, Julia, and Aly.

A birthday celebration with, Tom, center standing, sons Greg, left, and Frank, right, and grandsons, seated, Thomas and David.

Greg, standing, with David, Francie, and Thomas at the 2010 Oklahoma Hall of Fame Banquet & Induction Ceremony to honor Judy upon her induction.

Attending the 2010 Oklahoma Hall of Fame to celebrate Judy's induction were granddaughters Caroline, Claire, and Liza.

Greg, Tom, Jenny, Judy and Laura at Laura's Debutante Ball.

Francie's Debutante Ball, from left: David, Thomas, Tom, Francie, Judy, and Greg.

Tom and Judy with daughters Jenny, left, and Laura, second from right.

Back row, Tom, Malia, and Judy with, front row, Julia, Emma, and Frank aboard *I Love Rewards*, named for Love's Repeat Buyers Program.

Caroline, Francie, and Malia.

The Love Family celebrates Tom and Judy's 50th wedding anniversary.

Claire, Liza, Caroline, and Laura.

David, Francie, Greg, Lisa, and Thomas.

Aly, Jenny and John Meyer.

Frank, Emma, Julia, and Malia.

THE LOVE FAMILY, 2018

Caroline and Gabe Ikard.

David, Claire, Caroline, Laura, Liza, and Thomas.

Close friends of Tom and Judy Love throw an 80th birthday celebration.

Annual Family meeting 2016

David Love with tire crew.

David, Greg and Thomas Love

The Love girls in Aspen.

Claire Cameron, BMCHS graduation.

Emma and
Julia Love

Emma, Julia, Liza,
Aly, and Caroline.

Jenny Meyer, Frank Love, Laura Love

Frank, Malia, Judy and Laura Love

Francie and Joe Koop

Greg and Francie

Love Family at Francie and Joe's wedding

Frank and Malia Love

Judy with Thomas and David

Frank, Emma, Julia and Malia

Frank, Jenny, Judy, Tom, Laura, Greg

Frank and Malia Love, Caroline Ikard, Aly Meyer

Lisa and Greg Love

257

Monthly family birthday celebrations.

Jenny and John Meyer, Lisa and Greg Love

Jenny, John, Lisa, Greg, Laura, Judy, Tom, Caroline and Thomas.

Jenny Meyer, Laura Love

Jenny, Aly and John Meyer

John and Jenny Meyer

John, Jenny and Aly Meyer

Judy and Tom Love

The Love Family in Aspen, Colorado.

Tom Love

Lisa and Greg

Laura and Malia

Laura, Claire, Liza, Judy and Caroline

Laura, Tom, Jenny and Aly

Francie, Liza, Tom, Claire and Caroline

Thomas Love, Greg Love, Francie Koop, David Love

Thomas and David Love

Love's 50th Anniversary Celebration

Greg, Francie and Joe

Thomas, Tom and David

Tom and Judy Love
with Laura Love

Tom Love, Aly Meyer

Tom and Judy, 80th Birthday Celebration.

The Love Family "loves" the Oklahoma City Thunder.

Facing page: Tom and Judy at book signing.

INDEX

Tom and Judy with Brenda and Tom McDaniel on their way to an OU football game.

New Year's celebration with Jay Johnston, George Jay, Tom, and Paul Brou.

Judy and Tom, far right, on a trip with friends to Istanbul, the largest city in Turkey.

Tom and Judy with friends who hosted a birthday celebration for Judy.

LOVE'S: FIFTY-FIVE YEARS OF A FAMILY'S ENTERPRISE